INVESTIGATING
DISCIPLINARY
LITERACY

INVESTIGATING DISCIPLINARY LITERACY

A FRAMEWORK FOR COLLABORATIVE PROFESSIONAL LEARNING

CHRISTINA L. DOBBS

JACY IPPOLITO

MEGIN CHARNER-LAIRD

HARVARD EDUCATION PRESS

CAMBRIDGE, MASSACHUSETTS

Paperback ISBN 978-1-68253-068-9
Library Edition ISBN 978-1-68253-069-6

Library of Congress Cataloging-in-Publication Data
Names: Dobbs, Christina L., author. | Ippolito, Jacy, author. | Charner-Laird, Megin, author.
Title: Investigating disciplinary literacy : a framework for collaborative professional learning / Christina L. Dobbs, Jacy Ippolito, Megin Charner-Laird.
Description: Cambridge, Massachusetts : Harvard Education Press, [2017] | Includes bibliographical references and index.
Identifiers: LCCN 2017013628| ISBN 9781682530689 (pbk.) | ISBN 9781682530696 (library edition)
Subjects: LCSH: Professional learning communities. | Teachers–Training of. | Language arts–Correlation with content subjects. | Inquiry-based learning.
Classification: LCC LB1731 .D583 2017 | DDC 370.71/1–dc23 LC record available at https://lccn.loc.gov/2017013628

Published by Harvard Education Press,
an imprint of the Harvard Education Publishing Group

Harvard Education Press
8 Story Street
Cambridge, MA 02138

Cover Design: Endpaper Studio
Cover Photo: Tetra Images/Getty Images

The typefaces used in this book are Classica Pro, Open Sans, and Clasica Slab.

CONTENTS

FOREWORD

IF YOU ARE INTERESTED in moving students' literacy to the next level, then this book is for you. If you want someone to tell you exactly how to do that, then this book is not for you.

For some readers, this may feel a little like going to a doctor with a pressing health issue and being told that you need to make lifestyle changes rather than taking that magic pill you were hoping for. On the one hand, the magic pill or the clear prescription for high-level literacy is so appealing. On the other hand, the magic pill can have unintended side effects and doesn't account for the inevitable variations in context among people and environments, thus, working for some better than others. And sometimes, as is the case here, the magic prescription with its just-do-this-and-that clarity doesn't exist.

While I confess that I often wish for easy fixes, I also have a strong suspicion of them when it comes to difficult challenges. Once I get over my disappointment that the solution may be every bit as complex as the problem, it can be rather liberating to take control of my own destiny, particularly if there is some expert assistance available to adapt to fit my situation.

The authors of this book, Christina Dobbs, Jacy Ippolito, and Megin Charner-Laird, offer just the right kind of expert assistance, grounded in both research and practice. They know what they're talking about, and they also know that context matters. Thus, they pose a mix of conceptual grounding and practical things to do, with their seven-step framework sitting in the middle of the "why" and the "how" as synthetic glue. They offer all that to you and trust you to make it work in your context.

Their framework is a treasure trove in its own right. Even if you are interested in some focus other than disciplinary literacy, I'd recommend the book as a helpful antidote to some other long-standing plagues of school improvement, including blaming teachers, "collaboration," and "professional development" with little learning to show for lots of resources invested, and data-based inquiry that wanes at the point of action.

Instead, Dobbs, Ippolito, and Charner-Laird suggest that we respect and build from teachers' expertise, design based on what we know about effective professional learning, and rely on a mix of teacher leadership, collaborative structures, and experimentation to move from inquiry to action. In short, they give you the best of what we know about how to actually change practice and center teachers firmly as the agents rather than the targets of change. How refreshing. And more important, how potentially potent.

WHY DISCIPLINARY LITERACY?

Before reading this book, I hadn't heard of "disciplinary literacy." I had taught English and Humanities to middle school and high school students in two countries and three states. I had been a literacy coach to middle school teachers in Boston. And I had served as principal of a secondary school in which we taught reading strategies across the curriculum. I love literacy. But *disciplinary* literacy? It's counterintuitive for me, particularly in the twenty-first century.

Shouldn't we be getting away from disciplines? Most lists of "twenty-first-century skills" emphasize things like teamwork and problem solving, and there is increasing focus in schools on "real world" projects that are interdisciplinary in nature. Subjects in silos seem so twentieth century. . . .

Dobbs, Ippolito, and Charner-Laird quickly convinced me that the emergent field of disciplinary literacy is not about content silos, but about communication. Put simply, it's about how experts in various domains communicate. How do mathematicians, musicians, biologists, historians, and poets make sense of the world and relay that? What does it sound like when they talk to each other? What texts do they draw on? How do they use print, images, and other media to engage others with their ideas?

Disciplinary literacy makes sense because it puts communication in context rather than asking students to engage in the artifices of school. Very twenty-first century.

I'm drawn to the concept of disciplinary literacy for three reasons. First and foremost: power. When we treat students as mathematicians, scientists, artists, and writers, and when we make transparent for them the manners and modes of interpreting, challenging, and persuading, we unlock the worlds of professions and expertise and hand students the keys. These keys are particularly powerful for those students whose primary access to them is through school.

Second: disciplinary literacy connects with teachers' existing strengths and builds from them. Many a time, I have heard the refrain, "But I am not an English teacher!" in response to requests or demands to teach reading and/or writing across the curriculum. My rather impatient internal response has been, "Yes, but that doesn't let you off the hook for teaching reading/writing!" Spoken like an English teacher. Turns out, I was right, and so were the refrainers. Disciplinary literacy meets content teachers where they are–as masters of their disciplines– and asks them to apprentice students. While this approach requires teachers to learn some things, like how to make explicit what is ingrained and often easy for them, that learning builds from expertise rather than ignoring it. That is a much more enjoyable and efficacious way to learn.

Third: the pursuit of disciplinary literacy as described by Dobbs, Ippolito, and Charner-Laird is well positioned to produce positive organizational side effects. Their inquiry process is a means of building productive teams and organizations with healthy habits and mind-sets. It is less about producing best practices than about learning for children, adults, and the organization.

BUILDING DISCIPLINARY LITERACY

Dobbs, Ippolito, and Charner-Laird argue that building disciplinary literacy is fundamentally an "adaptive" enterprise, not a technical one. In other words, there is a level of uncertainty about how to do it, and it requires shifts in mind-sets and beliefs, as well as practice. Adaptive work, as described by my colleague Ronald Heifetz, by definition cannot be captured in a technical manual or cookbook approach.

I agree with the authors' assessment that this is adaptive work, and I appreciate their deft provision of ingredients and suggestions without prescriptive recipes. Some of those ingredients will sound familiar to many readers–for example, professional learning communities, inquiry, and teacher leadership– and what you will find here is: (a) how to do them well, and (b) how they can be more powerful together than apart. While that alone would be a contribution, I find even more valuable three uncommon suggestions from the authors.

First, pay attention to beginnings and endings. Especially endings. While Dobbs, Ippolito, and Charner-Laird spend time helping readers be thoughtful about how to venture into disciplinary literacy, including "seductive traps" to avoid, their more radical notion is that the initiative should have a decided end point. How cathartic!

"Action space" is another of the radical ideas they invite readers to consider. What kind of "space" is there for the kind of "action" you seek in your organization right now? If your answer is something like "Space? What space?" or "Did you mean action outside the sixty-seven initiatives we are currently doing?" then the authors suggest that you ponder a few more questions before deciding whether and when to dive into disciplinary literacy.

While resonant with my own understanding of improvement, Dobbs, Ippolito, and Charner-Laird's frame of experimentation is rare in practice. They encourage quick loops of inquiry that include small changes and experiments designed, tested, and analyzed by teachers. As you read the book, note how tightly focused the examples of inquiry are–teachers are not tackling the whole of disciplinary literacy, but instead are engaging some specific puzzle or problem related to student learning. In my experience, it is the focus that feels almost too small that leads to actual learning. Improvement is less the end product of arduous inquiry than a series of micro-moments intentionally designed and learned from.

This book fundamentally is about agency, building from what you have, designing intentionally, and learning collaboratively and continuously. It is about discipline as both context and approach. As context, literacy is situated within disciplines as a way of moving past the plateaus many of us have encountered after teaching what the authors call "intermediate" strategies. Discipline as approach is well captured by Boston surgeon Atul Gawande in his book, *The Checklist Manifesto: How to Get Things Right*:

> What is needed, however, isn't just that people working together be nice to each other. It is discipline. Discipline is hard–harder than trustworthiness and skill and perhaps even than selflessness. We are by nature flawed and inconstant creatures. We can't even keep from snacking between meals. We are not built for discipline. We are built for novelty and excitement, not for careful attention to detail. Discipline is something we have to work at.

Dobbs, Ippolito, and Charner-Laird show how educators can move from "being-nice-to-each-other" collaborations to disciplined inquiry. Experts do not always have answers, but they have great questions, and Dobbs, Ippolito, and Charner-Laird offer some of both. While disciplinary literacy is plainly something "we have to work at," it is also clearly worth doing for and with students.

Literacy is freedom, hope, and power. Through the lens of disciplinary literacy, may this book help you unlock more of the incredible potential in yourself, your colleagues, and your students.

Elizabeth A. City
Senior Lecturer on Education
Faculty Director, Doctor of Educational Leadership Program
Harvard Graduate School of Education

INTRODUCTION

As FORMER TEACHERS, reading specialists, and literacy coaches, we know first-hand how excellent professional development projects can bolster teacher and student learning. Alternately, professional learning can be a deadly waste of time, money, and energy if not carefully constructed. While we—Christina Dobbs, Jacy Ippolito, and Megin Charner-Laird—now spend the bulk of our time teaching in higher-education classrooms, we also focus a good deal of our professional and academic energy on designing, implementing, and studying successful professional learning endeavors. We're fascinated by the question of how to authentically build and support professional learning projects to increase teacher and student learning, especially student reading, writing, and communication skills. In many ways, this book answers this question, based on both our professional experiences and academic research. But we knew that answering this question in a general or mainly theoretical manner might be of little use to those who matter the most to us—teachers on the ground, working daily with young people in schools. Instead, we knew that focus and utility were key. In order to provide these elements and use our own areas of expertise, we have grounded our thinking about professional learning in the particular case of *disciplinary literacy professional learning*.

More than a half-dozen years ago, we began turning our collective attention to the newly emerging field of *disciplinary literacy*, or the study of how both experts and novice students read, write, and communicate within specific disciplinary fields. What does it mean to engage in disciplinary literacy work? One might start to answer this question by considering how discipline-specific experts read, write, and communicate similarly or differently depending on their field. For example, which ways of thinking, communicating, and working do artists, biologists, historians, and statisticians share? Which ways of thinking are different? At the heart of disciplinary literacy is a deep understanding of key differences between disciplines in how knowledge is constructed and how it is

1

transmitted within and across academic and vocational fields. Building on these understandings, teachers might begin to consider how best to induct students into these same disciplinary subcultures, helping students slowly gain access and insight into various disciplinary fields through the advanced language, ways of thinking, and ways of working associated with each discipline. In this way, teachers serve as guides, introducing and inviting students into the communities of artists, biologists, historians, or statisticians by teaching them the language and analytic approaches specific to those disciplines.

At the outset of the twenty-first century, teachers and leaders in US schools are grappling with how to prepare students to meet the challenges of a more global economy. Workplace demands, college expectations, and new standards for preK–12 education are reshaping education nationwide. We believe that a more deliberate focus on disciplinary literacy instruction is necessary in order to support students as they forge ahead to face these challenges. And while new research about disciplinary literacy is being published (some of which we review in the first chapters of this book), little is currently known or shared about how to effectively engage teachers in the complex professional learning they need to teach in ways that support disciplinary literacy.

Disciplinary literacy professional learning is different from professional learning writ large. To truly understand the nuances of one's own discipline, and how to teach the reading, writing, and communication patterns of disciplinary insiders (experts in their fields), teachers must embark on an individual and collaborative journey. Ideally, teams of teachers must uncover the ways in which they were inducted into various disciplines and develop strategies to best apprentice their own students in beginning to do this disciplinary work. Moreover, many teachers go into fields for which they already feel some great affinity or expertise. Helping students who may not feel similarly about their disciplines requires a great deal of strategic thinking and action.

Thus, we argue in this book that the disciplinary literacy instruction that is so sorely needed in our twenty-first-century schools depends largely on the quality of instruction that students receive and thus depends largely on the quality and kind of professional learning experiences that support such instruction. But that kind of professional learning is neither simple nor quick.

In this book, we provide a road map for teams of secondary educators and leaders to build their own capacity to provide disciplinary literacy instruction. While many articles and books have emerged in the past twenty years purporting to address the challenges facing adolescents in literacy, we take a fundamentally different approach here. We set out not to solve the myriad content-area literacy instructional challenges found in every middle and high school nationwide. Instead, we describe an approach in which teachers and leaders can identify and craft context-specific solutions, to tinker effectively toward a better marriage of content and literacy teaching and learning, in order to help students develop the disciplinary literacy skills and habits that will propel them into more advanced work.

We have developed this road map, our multistep framework, across the last ten years, as we have worked closely with a number of different schools and districts to improve adolescent literacy outcomes for their students by focusing on disciplinary literacy. We are university professors who have previously worked in K–12 schools and who now split our time between supporting preservice teachers and helping in-service teachers across grade levels. In this book we hope to use what we have learned about literacy and professional learning to help teachers find and build tools to improve their instruction. We have sometimes been frustrated at the general ways that most professional learning opportunities for teachers tend to ignore the priorities of teachers and to devalue their knowledge and expertise.

So, years ago, when a high school asked us to lead a literacy initiative, we began to think about how to combine current knowledge of literacy research with more lasting and powerful models of professional learning in ways that could support a particular school context. Since then, we have worked with a variety of schools, some with many resources and some with far fewer, some large and some small. In each case, we find that when teachers deliberately and strategically collaborate to improve disciplinary literacy outcomes, we see meaningful changes in teachers' instructional practices. Over time and across many collaborative initiatives with teachers, we have piloted and refined a framework for collaborative professional learning about disciplinary literacy to support teachers over time. We will describe this framework in more detail throughout the book and hear from many participants in the projects we have supported in the past decade.

This book is not filled with quick fixes, which are always hit or miss at best, depending on your own school structure, faculty, or student population. Instead, this book honors and calls upon your own expertise, and supports you as you enter into and refine your own iterative professional learning process.

Therefore, we have written this book with several types of readers in mind. We see this book primarily in the hands of teachers, school leaders, and district and state leaders who are eager to help disciplinary literacy instruction take hold in schools to raise student achievement in a variety of content areas. As the need to embrace disciplinary literacy grows, teachers and leaders need practical advice about how to tackle disciplinary literacy professional learning *now*. This book contains our best advice to undertake that work. It is aimed most directly at helping educators to successfully tackle the challenge of bringing disciplinary literacy instruction to their specific classrooms and schools. However, this book is also useful for educational consultants, researchers, and those teaching in higher education and preservice teacher-preparation programs. This book may serve as an excellent guide and jumping-off point for those who are considering how best to support others in designing and studying effective literacy-based professional learning projects. If we are to truly see a proliferation of authentic, effective, ongoing professional learning around disciplinary literacy instruction, then we will need a wide variety of educators engaged in the endeavor from different vantage points.

With these different audiences in mind, we have divided the book into two major sections. The first part, "Bringing Together Disciplinary Literacy and Professional Learning," comprising three chapters, provides foundational background information that readers may need or wish to review, in order to support later practical chapters focused on how to design and implement professional learning projects. The first three chapters, respectively, review the emerging field of disciplinary literacy research and teaching, foundational elements of effective professional learning, and the possible design of *disciplinary literacy professional learning* projects. This first part of the book ends, in chapter 3, with an introduction to our seven-step framework for how readers might design and implement a disciplinary literacy professional learning project.

The second part, "Designing and Enacting Disciplinary Literacy Professional Learning," begins with chapter 4. Each of the chapters 4 through 10 are devoted to different phases of the seven-step design and implementation process—all with an eye toward the kinds of context-specific decisions and modifications required to ensure that the professional learning work is tailored to the teachers and students in particular schools and districts. These chapters are process focused and filled with practical suggestions for how to engage various professional stakeholders. We move from early investigative and needs assessment work to design phases, early implementation, and finally refinement and scaling of the work. These practical chapters include potential supports such as discussion-based protocols to use when talking with various community members, questions to guide leadership team discussions and decisions, potential pitfalls to avoid, and Snapshots of Practice highlighting disciplinary literacy work from schools that illustrate the various steps in our design and implementation process.

The snapshots of disciplinary literacy throughout the book come directly from teachers and leaders with whom we have worked, each of whom has successfully navigated their way through unique, complex disciplinary literacy professional learning initiatives.[1] Many of the snapshots we include come from a lengthy project we worked on for several years at Brookline High School in Brookline, Massachusetts, which had many participants across four years of collaboration. You will also see snapshots from projects in other schools and districts, including Boston and Acton-Boxborough. Below, we briefly describe each of the disciplinary literacy initiatives mentioned in snapshots throughout the text in chapters 4–10. We, the authors of the book, participated in a variety ways in each project. The size and scope of the projects varied greatly, because each was tailored to the particular needs and resources of their schools and districts.

Brookline High School's Content-Area Reading Initiative. Brookline High School's Content-Area Reading Initiative (CRI) was designed as a four-year project, which allowed for a total of six teams of high school content-area teachers, specialists, and librarians to explore a wide variety of literacy-related domains (e.g., academic language, vocabulary, discussion, writing, and so on). The first cohort of three teams comprised English, social studies, and world languages teachers, and they collaborated for the initial two years of the project. The second cohort of three teams worked together for the last two years of the project, and they represented the math and science departments, as well as a cross-role team (team "Hybrid") focused on meeting the needs of students with learning differences. Structural features of the project included summer institutes, weekly small-team meetings led by designated teacher leaders, quarterly cross-team "days away" (where the teams would meet off-site, out of their school building, to share new learning), and consulting coaches who led professional learning and coached teams throughout.

OneDot. "*One Dorchester*" was a four-year, school-driven effort among three schools—Boston Collegiate Charter School, Cristo Rey Boston High School, and the Jeremiah Burke High School—to learn from each other in the quest to improve student outcomes. By sharing best practices and defining high-quality teaching and learning, this first-ever formal partnership between Boston-based district, charter, and Catholic schools built the capacity of teachers in all three schools to create transformational learning communities focused on equity, while increasing the number of students in Dorchester who were prepared to enter and succeed in college. Activities for each discipline-based team included participating in professional development and accessing materials related to the Common Core State Standards; observing each other in the classroom; engaging in collective analysis of student work; developing rubrics and assessments; surfacing ideas on instructional and curricular shifts to respond to student data; creating a common vision for high-quality work; and learning more about how to elicit high-quality work from students. The Lynch Foundation funded One Dorchester from July 2012 through July 2016; Gene Thompson-Grove from the School Reform Initiative (SRI) coordinated the effort. As part of her work, she asked us to lead a summer literacy institute with participating teacher teams designed to build disciplinary literacy knowledge.

Boston Green Academy Tenth-Grade Instructional Improvement Project.
The BGA Instructional Improvement Project was a yearlong project with tenth-grade teachers across content areas at Boston Green Academy. The school was working hard to improve student achievement, so the project was designed to support teachers in enhancing their instruction to further that effort. A team of core teachers from humanities, literacy, math, and environmental science came together with specialist teachers from special education to focus on ensuring that all students were refining their literacy skills in the disciplines. The team, led by a teacher leader and with outside expertise from Christina as a consultant, met weekly to identify inquiry areas and design and evaluate new instructional practices.

Acton-Boxborough Disciplinary Literacy Initiative.
The Acton-Boxborough Disciplinary Literacy Initiative was also designed as a four-year project, allowing for a total of twelve teams of middle and high school content-area teachers, specialists, and librarians to explore a wide variety of literacy-related domains (e.g., academic language, vocabulary, discussion, writing, and so on).

The teams also collaborated within cohorts, with each cohort of six teams (three from the middle school and three from the high school per cohort) spending roughly two years engaged in the initiative. Teams comprised both content-specific and cross-content area teachers and specialists. Teachers and specialists across all academic departments participated, including librarians. Monthly small-team meetings, monthly larger-group meetings, and regular delivery of new content from consulting coaches were stable features throughout the project. Other design features varied by cohort, with one cohort holding summer institutes, while the other received more direct professional development during the academic year. Both cohorts engaged in peer observation and instructional rounds as part of their work. Last, several emerging teacher leaders from the first cohort led monthly meetings and study groups for the second cohort.

Brookline Middle School Disciplinary Literacy Initiative.   This disciplinary literacy initiative is ongoing, and in the first years of implementation. The project began with four cross-content area teams of teachers, with each team representing a different middle school in the district. The goal is to mirror Brookline's CRI project in its four-year structure, with teams collaborating for roughly two years at a stretch, and new cohorts of cross-content area teachers from other middle schools in the district joining the initiative during year three. Designated teacher leaders guide the teams of teachers, and they meet several times per month to collaboratively inquire into new disciplinary literacy instructional practices. The teams all come together for new professional learning, led by consulting coaches, roughly five times during the school year, and then once per summer (but not necessarily as part of a summer institute format).

We include the Snapshots of Practice in the book to honor the important work of these teachers and leaders, to bring to life aspects of our seven-step design and implementation process, and to help readers imagine some of the many different possible paths to success.

Most importantly, this book is designed to be a resource guide and source for deeper reflection when designing and implementing a disciplinary literacy professional learning initiative. This is not a cookbook, filled with exacting recipes that should be unwaveringly followed. Instead, this book is a reflective tool, crafted to help teachers and leaders consider the pros and cons of different decisions when designing and engaging in professional learning. To that end, some readers (perhaps those early in their thinking about disciplinary literacy professional learning) may wish to read the book chapter by chapter, slowly building an understanding of the entire process of designing, implementing, and refining a professional learning initiative. Other readers with more experience in designing professional learning (perhaps those in the midst of their own project) might skim the early design chapters and then focus more closely on the later implementation and scaling chapters. Regardless of how you personally choose to navigate through the text, we do encourage all readers to spend some time reviewing the first three chapters. The early chapters form the theoretical foundation supporting the practical advice that appears in later chapters.

We hope that you enjoy reading this book as much as we enjoyed writing it. We truly value the time we have spent with our partner schools and teachers, learning together about disciplinary literacy. We hope that these pages convey some of the same collaborative energy and enthusiasm that we feel every time we engage in that kind of collective learning. In creating this book, we learned a great deal from one another and from our partners, as we clarified and synthesized years' worth of thinking about disciplinary literacy professional learning work. We hope that this book sparks just as much thinking and good work for you.

Bringing Together Disciplinary Literacy and Professional Learning

CHAPTER 1

The Challenge of Disciplinary Literacy

DILEMMAS FROM THE CLASSROOM

- A high school history teacher worries that her students are not effectively reading primary source texts filled with antiquated vocabulary and difficult sentence structure. She wrestles with whether focusing on and explicitly teaching the difficult vocabulary are worth the time, given that students may not run across those particular words again soon.
- A biology teacher struggles as students glean little meaning from their textbook, a dense text with layers and layers of unfamiliar words and figures arranged in complex hierarchies. She considers whether their time spent reading the text might be better used if she presented the material herself via PowerPoint.
- A middle school math teacher promises himself nearly every day that he will engage students in rich conversations and real-world problem-solving dilemmas, yet he regretfully ends more classes than he cares to admit with students copying problems from the whiteboard and calculating independently at their desks.
- A Spanish teacher is anxious because, though the students are learning new Spanish vocabulary, they are reluctant to talk to each other using these new

words. She tries different strategies to help make this expectation of talk an everyday habit in her classroom.

- An English/language arts teacher is trying to help her students to use more literary language in their discussions about class texts and to respond to each other, rather than relying on her to always call on students. She is disheartened on days when she feels that students have not had the unique experience of participating in a deep, free-form discussion about literature.

These challenges and many others are not uncommon within and across middle and high school content-area classrooms. They are a mixture of challenges specific to each particular content area and challenges that cut across subject areas. While many teachers struggle with these sorts of dilemmas alone, most professional learning experiences are not designed to simultaneously support teachers in individual classrooms as well as across departments and grade levels. This book focuses on the ways in which secondary content-area teachers *can* work and learn together in order to support students as they develop the specific ways of reading, writing, and communicating required in different content-area classrooms. Yet this is no easy task.

Before we detail the ways in which teams of educators can productively learn about and teach content and literacy in deeply integrated ways, we must first explain what we mean by *adolescent literacy*, *disciplinary literacy*, and *professional learning*—the conceptual pillars upon which this book and our own ways of working have been built. First, let's turn our attention to adolescent literacy and the challenges facing adolescents in school.

THE CHALLENGE OF ADOLESCENT LITERACY

While US educators have been thinking about the particular language, literacy, and learning needs of adolescents for over a hundred years, the past twenty years have seen a resurgence in research and practice related to bolstering adolescents' reading, writing, and communication skills.[1] Rightly so, as adolescents face a unique set of learning challenges in middle and high school classrooms.

As students move into adolescence, their school classes become more separate and self-contained. They might spend roughly an hour in math class, an hour in English, an hour in Spanish, an hour in US history, and so on, until the day's end. Some blocks of time might be longer, some shorter; daily schedules and content-area classes often rotate, leaving both teachers and students constantly moving from class to class, subject to subject, assignment to assignment. This constant movement means that, unlike elementary teachers, secondary teachers focus almost exclusively on their own particular content-area goals. Thus, secondary teachers are typically trained as specialists, experts in the disciplines they will be teaching. This focus on the disciplines, with all of their associated discipline-specific vocabulary, texts, and tasks, means that the various classes each place unique literacy demands on students. All involve reading, writing, speaking, and listening in particular ways, which teachers and students do not always explicitly discuss.

This is especially problematic for high school-aged adolescents, who are often moving among a number of content-area classes per day and have to rapidly adopt and then shift discipline-specific ways of communicating. Imagine the effect on a student whose literacy skills are not strong—moving from class to class every hour, with the content, language, and literacy expectations constantly shifting, leaving the student without a robust working knowledge of what to do. These struggles have lasting effects on a student's sense of competence, school achievement, and prospects for postsecondary education.[2] Having strong literacy skills in various disciplinary classrooms opens doors for students. But too often, teacher preparation programs do not show preservice teachers how they might effectively apprentice students into disciplinary ways of knowing. The particular ways of being literate in various content areas necessitate new strategies for how to address literacy–preparation that content-area teachers rarely experience.

In addition to these high demands in literacy, teachers must also attend to the variety of skills involved in being highly literate in the twenty-first century; many content-area teachers lack training here as well. Literacy includes all the facets of reading, writing, speaking, and listening, along with typical component skills like vocabulary and discussion, as well as more modern skills in areas such as digital literacy. In this book, we will refer to these various component skills as "domains," as we describe the many ways teachers focus on improving literacy in their classrooms and the related professional learning supports that help teachers gain domain- and discipline-specific knowledge.

In an era when adolescent literacy achievement is a cause for much concern, increasing attention is being paid to the ways that literacy demands shift and change as students progress through the grades and into more specialized classes.[3] Recently, this evolving work has taken the form of disciplinary literacy instruction—helping adolescents achieve the sophisticated reading, writing, and communication skills necessary to participate in disciplinary communities. In other words, when students gain disciplinary literacy skills, they learn how to communicate like novice historians or mathematicians, or burgeoning experts from many other disciplines. While the Common Core State Standards, and many researchers and policy makers, have recently called for a shift toward disciplinary literacy teaching and learning, it is difficult to find guidance about how middle and high school educators might work collaboratively to tackle the task of shifting to a disciplinary literacy way of working.

While we agree with the recent call for a shift toward disciplinary literacy instruction, our own research and experience have taught us that adopting a disciplinary literacy teaching and learning orientation is not a simple, overnight process.[4] Nor is it a process that is best undertaken alone, or a stance that is adopted after hearing briefly from outside experts. Instead, we believe this work takes time and close collaboration. In order to develop a disciplinary literacy stance in teaching, we focus on how teachers might engage in effective professional learning to learn about and support the adoption and refinement of disciplinary literacy instructional practices. This collaborative kind of work, we believe, holds great promise in supporting teachers, such as the ones we describe in the opening vignettes. By collaborating to uncover their own discipline-specific ways of reading, writing, and communicating, and then crafting new instructional practices to model those habits for students, teachers can bring sophisticated literacy skills to students in order to improve their disciplinary knowledge and achievement.

DISCIPLINARY LITERACY: AN INTRODUCTION

The concept of disciplinary literacy began to receive widespread attention around 2008, in part due to the publication of Timothy Shanahan and Cynthia Shanahan's landmark article, "Teaching Disciplinary Literacy to Adolescents: Rethinking Content-Area Literacy."[5] The piece argued that literacy skills become increasingly more complex, sophisticated, and discipline specific as students move through the grades and into increasingly varied disciplines, like biology, calculus, physics, or psychology. The Shanahans defined disciplinary literacy as the skills used to read, write, speak, and listen that are particular to each discipline. While this sounds simple at first, like many breakthrough ideas, the practical implications of adopting a disciplinary literacy lens are more complex. Disciplinary literacy instruction asks all educators to carefully consider and explicitly teach the ways in which different disciplines build and share knowledge, processes that are not always so transparent to those both within and outside of specific disciplines.

The claims in the Shanahans' 2008 article were soon echoed in the Common Core State Standards for adolescent students: "Literacy standards for grade 6 and above are predicated on teachers of ELA, history/social studies, science, and technical subjects using their content area expertise to help students meet the particular challenges of reading, writing, speaking, listening, and language in their respective fields."[6]

The Common Core State Standards have helped to launch the current national shift toward teaching disciplinary literacy in middle and high schools, and many schools are trying to address the sorts of challenges described at the beginning of this chapter. In doing so, they attempt to raise literacy achievement levels for all students.

Since the Shanahans' paper in 2008, dozens of articles and books about disciplinary literacy have been published.[7] Fueled by growing research and advocacy, the disciplinary literacy movement has gained traction and attention. But the movement did not materialize out of thin air. The shift toward disciplinary literacy emerged from a one-hundred-year history of frustration with approaches to *content-area literacy* that failed to produce hoped-for results. When considering adopting and refining disciplinary literacy instructional practices, it can first be helpful to look back and understand how we got here and where secondary schools might currently stand with teaching students to read, write, and communicate.

A quick history: Content-area literacy

Initially, the notion of reading successfully in the content areas was framed as *content-area reading instruction*—a way of teaching cognitive strategies across various content-area classrooms in order to promote reading comprehension.[8] The theory held that schools could explicitly teach these comprehension strategies to students in different content-area classrooms to help them successfully understand history, math, and science texts. The emphasis on strategy use in content classrooms led to calls for "every teacher [to be] a teacher of reading," and this implementation would theoretically support students to read more effectively in content-area classrooms.[9]

For example, imagine a high school US history class reading a textbook chapter and primary sources related to the Civil War. A school taking a content-area reading approach to improving students' reading skills might focus on teaching explicit, but general strategies for improving reading, such as making strong text-based inferences, determining which main ideas are most important in a text, or asking students to make connections to other time periods, texts, and their own lives. Often the strategies fall into one of seven broad categories of cognitive routines that good readers presumably use fluidly and automatically: making connections, generating questions, visualizing, making inferences, determining importance, synthesizing, and monitoring or fixing up comprehension.[10] The teacher would have encouraged students to use these general strategies, useful in many contexts inside and outside social studies, to establish strong general reading routines.

This approach to reading instruction at the secondary level has had modest success, with research demonstrating that some explicit reading instruction focused on comprehension strategies can improve students' understanding of texts across content areas.[11] Additional studies point specifically to how strategy instruction was used to support struggling readers with content-area reading.[12] Yet, content-area reading instruction alone has not produced widespread academic achievement for adolescents, and some secondary teachers and literacy researchers have wondered whether the limits of this instruction prevent it from fully preparing adolescents to meet college and workplace literacy demands.[13]

Not only has strategy-based instruction failed to prove effective across the board, many content-area teachers have resisted the incorporation of these generic reading strategies into their own classrooms.[14] After all, teaching an entire course in physics, split into fifty-minute increments across a semester or year, is daunting enough. Adding literacy instruction into the mix could be overwhelming. Plus, most secondary teachers have had little if any preparation in how to teach reading and how to incorporate general reading strategies into subject areas that vary widely. Though many teachers might acknowledge the importance of students' reading skills in successfully navigating their content-area classes, many teachers feel unprepared to support students in reading and writing texts in particular content areas, a problem that has persisted throughout the era of content-area reading instruction.[15]

Perhaps the most salient reason teachers resisted content-area reading instruction is the lack of fit between the generic literacy strategies being recommended to math, science, and social studies teachers and the discipline-specific reading, writing, and communication practices particular to those content areas.[16] Content areas are themselves disciplines, with nuanced and particularized ways of knowing and reading that generic strategies cannot address. With secondary teachers being trained as experts in their disciplines and disciplinary ways of thinking, it makes great sense to then appeal to that disciplinary training and suggest that the literacy skills embedded in content-area classes must also be more closely connected to disciplinary ways of knowing and communicating. Thus, the recent concept of disciplinary literacy, that each of the disciplines demands unique routines and strategies from readers, has pushed both teachers and researchers to consider a shift away from content-area reading. Instead of focusing on cross-cutting, generic reading and communication strategies, we are now witnessing the spread of a much more appealing (to secondary teachers) shift toward disciplinary literacy instruction.

What is disciplinary literacy?

Thus we return to 2008, when prominent researchers such as Tim Shanahan and Cynthia Shanahan and Elizabeth Birr Moje began popularizing the argument that adolescents' acquisition of advanced literacy skills would necessitate a shift in the instructional practice of teachers. Additionally, it could necessitate a shift in the way students enact reading, writing, speaking, and interpretation skills. For example, reading in a history class would require very different skills and dispositions compared to reading in a health classroom. To build these different literacy skills, and as students' coursework becomes increasingly specialized through middle and high school, their teachers would necessarily need to provide instruction in the ways of reading the texts of their disciplines. For instance, students in a science class must learn one set of literacy skills in order to understand a figure illustrating the citric acid cycle, while in an English class, they learn an altogether different set of skills to understand and interpret complex works of poetry.

In 2008, the Shanahans introduced a popular heuristic for understanding the increasing complexity of literacy demands over time, one we think is useful in our own work, even as we continue to expand and refine it in practice. Their disciplinary literacy pyramid has three parts: (1) the base of the pyramid–basic literacy skills; (2) the middle–intermediate literacy skills; and (3) the top–disciplinary literacy skills (see figure 1.1). Basic literacy skills are defined as those that young children learn as they begin learning to read and write, such as how to decode and spell basic words. Intermediate skills are the sorts of general comprehension strategies at the heart of the content-area reading movement. The notion is that as students develop basic fluency, learn to make strong inferences, and develop general academic vocabulary, these intermediate skills could become the focal point of content-area reading instruction and bolster students as they focus more on reading to learn (a shift from the basic literacy stages of learning to read). The last piece of the pyramid, and the new focus of the current field, is the disciplinary literacy tip of the pyramid, focusing on the sorts of literacy skills specific to particular disciplines, specialized to reflect the habits of the broader professional communities associated with each of the various content areas.

Returning to the earlier dilemma of teaching high school US history, if the teacher were to adopt a disciplinary literacy approach to supporting students' reading of textbooks and primary sources, she might not focus much on general comprehension strategies. Instead, the teacher would consider how best to model for her students the ways in which she reads historical texts, as a disciplinary insider trained as a historian. She would still be teaching the skills of comprehension, but in ways that are more closely connected to the ways historians

FIGURE 1.1   **The increasing specialization of literacy pyramid**

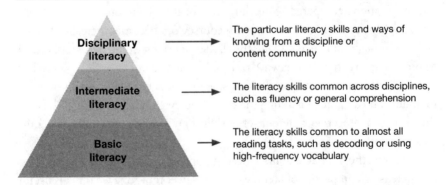

Source: Adapted from Timothy Shanahan and Cynthia Shanahan, "Teaching Disciplinary Literacy to Adolescents: Rethinking Content-Area Literacy," *Harvard Educational Review* 78 (2008): 44.

think and communicate. Rather than promoting simple or general inferences, a disciplinary literacy approach might focus on how issues of sourcing and bias influence the types of inferences one makes while reading and learning about history. She might simultaneously focus on how the language in the primary sources reveals clues about the time period, author's intent, or audience of the time, as opposed to simply learning vocabulary words to aid in comprehension or making connections across texts or from texts to one's own life. These more discipline-specific routines, or habits of mind, vary across content-area class-rooms. Furthermore, these variations, which range from slight to substantial, are the focus of disciplinary literacy approaches to supporting students' reading, writing, listening, and speaking skills across different content areas in ways consistent with those different disciplinary communities. Though entry into these communities begins in middle and high school with required classes such as calculus, chemistry, physics, and US and world history, strong skills in the literacy practices specific to these disciplines can help students gain access to these disciplinary communities in college and beyond, as they land in professional communities of expert engineers, physicists, diplomats, or scholars. (See table 1.1 for examples of how various disciplines differ in terms of the literacy demands they place on students.)

In order to equip students with these disciplinary literacy skills, the Shanahans, Moje, and other researchers and policy makers argue that teachers need to model the habits of mind and ways of reading and writing used by historians, mathematicians, and scientists.[17] Ultimately, this requires that teachers incorporate disciplinary literacy practices in their day-to-day lessons in order to better induct students into disciplinary communities and the discursive practices of those communities.

To begin mapping new instructional practices for secondary teachers, literacy researchers began documenting how experts in various professional fields, with particular disciplinary training, read differently from those in other disciplines. They documented how historians approached text by considering issues such as causality, sourcing, contextualization, and bias, while reading in mathematics was more focused on reason and the convergence of evidence.[18] Some saw these habits as a potential source of advanced achievement in the content areas. Others argued that the inclusion of disciplinary literacy in the content areas opens up opportunities for further work and study to *all* students in ways that promote social justice and more equitable opportunities.[19]

TABLE 1.1   Some examples of disciplinary differences*

	Habits of mind	Reading tasks and texts	Norms of presenting and writing
Social studies/ history	• Understanding bias • Corroborating information with a variety of sources	• *Text type*: Primary sources • *Text type*: Timelines • Comparing varied accounts of events	• Cause/effect essays • Oral presentations with a variety of media (e.g., video, photos)
Math	• Asking and answering questions using numbers and symbols • Persisting through problems, including when various strategies fail	• *Text type*: Graphs and figures • Information presented in symbols, pictures, or words • Rereading problems and tracking variables and given information	• Writing ideas, notes, and problem-solving steps • Writing proofs or other sequences • Discussing reasoning and decisions
English/ language arts	• Noticing and analyzing literary language such as symbolism or metaphor • Understanding various literary genres	• *Text type*: Novels and plays • *Text type*: Poetry • Placing read texts in a broader historical context	• Writing analytic essays with thesis statements and textual evidence • Writing various genres • Discussions of textual analysis
Science	• Understanding the purpose and process of the scientific method • Using parts-to-whole thinking to classify	• *Text type*: Informational texts • *Text type*: Graphs, figures, and charts • Looking for key terms that imply relationships	• Recording data and observations • Taking notes and recording problem-solving steps • Presenting research findings in formal ways such as papers or posters

*These are examples of different habits of mind, reading tasks, and norms of presenting and writing in disciplines; the lists are not meant to be comprehensive.

Policy makers, school leaders, and educational thinkers have latched onto the idea of disciplinary literacy because it holds promise to advance students' knowledge and skills within the disciplines, preparing them for higher education and life beyond. Teaching disciplinary literacy skills at the secondary level welcomes students into a community of scholars within each discipline they encounter, providing them with opportunities to build expertise, hone prefer-ences for further study, and lay the groundwork for future success within a cho-sen field. As the Shanahans note in a recent article:

> It [disciplinary literacy] says, "We in (fill in the field) want you to join us. We want to share with you our cognitive secrets, our ways of think-ing about the world, and how we solve problems. We want to count you as one of us." In doing that, it both holds out the promise of affiliation (connecting with others is a big motivator) and of greater competency with challenging tasks—not competency in being a kid (a student), but competency in being successful with the kinds of things that adults do.[20]

This idea of inviting students to see themselves as novice historians, biolo-gists, or literary critics is one filled with great potential for helping students see themselves as early practitioners of a particular discipline. Many books and arti-cles published recently are designed to support teachers as they help students learn these novice practices (see the appendix to this chapter, "A Few Notable Sources about Disciplinary Literacy," for a list of recent resources about disci-plinary literacy in specific content areas). However, though much importance and potential are attached to disciplinary literacy in research and policy realms, there is still a long way to go in order to fully implement this approach in middle and high school classrooms nationwide.

IMPLEMENTING DISCIPLINARY LITERACY INSTRUCTION

So, where do we go next? This book begins to provide some answers to prac-tice-based questions that have emerged as disciplinary literacy has gained popularity. Adopting and adapting disciplinary literacy teaching and learning practices is a complex enterprise, and schools must carefully consider how they might take on the challenge of implementing disciplinary literacy across a vari-ety of content areas. Schools cannot simply adopt a prepackaged disciplinary literacy curriculum or complete a onetime training session on the topic. Disci-plinary literacy instruction, we believe, is more complicated than what can be easily represented in such curricula or workshops. Instead, taking a disciplinary literacy stance toward content-area instruction means thinking about not only the scope and sequence of content but also the scope and sequence of the literacy skills needed to fully access that content. It requires the unearthing of one's own discipline-specific ways of reading, writing, and communicating, and then determining how to model those habits and ways of working for students. A simple curriculum package is unlikely to be the driver for change in instructional practice when it comes to disciplinary literacy, and an isolated workshop will not address the scope of content adequately to bring about real change.

In order to drive changes in instructional practice, teachers will almost certainly have to make instructional changes and invent new practices, sometimes in the context of their current curricula and sometimes as they are adopting new curricula. Teachers will need to work together, within and across content-area departments and grade levels, to do this complex work. Meanwhile, as secondary teachers are being asked to invent, adopt, and adapt disciplinary literacy practices, district- or school-level mandates to improve students' disciplinary literacy skills often come with little training or ongoing professional learning support.

We stand at a crossroads with regard to disciplinary literacy: Will this idea, which holds so much promise for teachers and, more importantly, for students' learning and futures, become a mainstay of teaching? Or will it fall by the wayside as yet another well-theorized but poorly implemented idea in education? While much work remains to be done in developing and researching effective disciplinary literacy instructional practices, much of the potential success of disciplinary literacy work lies in the practices that teachers themselves can develop if given the right tools and structures. Effective innovation, collaboration, and implementation among teachers at the department and school levels can provide teachers with the space to not only teach content but also address the literacy skills that help students access that content. Specifically, for teachers to realize the potential of disciplinary literacy, they must learn about, co-construct, and implement new strategies and approaches that unlock disciplinary literacy for their students.

Ultimately, then, the fate of disciplinary literacy rests on the shoulders of solid professional learning structures and routines that truly support teachers—a challenging proposition given the wide variability in professional learning structures and outcomes across schools and districts.[21] So, we must put into place meaningful professional learning structures to bring knowledge about disciplinary literacy to those who need it most. Right now, content-area teachers are often trained primarily in their particular disciplines, with little focus on literacy; meanwhile, literacy specialists are often not trained in particular content domains.[22] Disciplinary literacy is still a relatively new domain, and there are many strategies still to develop for teachers to implement, tweak, and ultimately integrate into their daily practice. Schools that hope to improve disciplinary literacy teaching and learning will need to be incredibly thoughtful about supporting teachers in building and sustaining robust professional learning structures to encourage this sort of learning. There is great potential for well-crafted, focused, professional learning experiences to be the key to teachers' implementation of disciplinary literacy in their classrooms.

Thus, it is those educators working at the intersection of exciting ideas about disciplinary literacy and on-the-ground professional learning realities that this book seeks to support. Our own research and professional development experiences have taught us that teachers have to work together to learn about, invent, digest, try out, discuss, and reflect on the implementation of new disciplinary literacy practices in their classrooms, a cycle that repeats itself. The ways in which teams of educators collaborate, support one another, and take collective risks will determine how disciplinary literacy practices will take hold or slip away from secondary classrooms around the globe in coming years. Will schools create the meaningful, in-depth learning opportunities teachers need in order to implement such wholesale changes in their instruction? Will teachers from various disciplines work together to develop or adapt literacy practices to encourage students to understand the differences in how disciplines construct knowledge? Or will teachers be left to interpret the ideas behind disciplinary literacy on their own, leading to varied interpretation, uneven implementation, and limited student achievement?

This book brings together the content of disciplinary literacy practices with the structures of professional learning that have proven to support implementation of these complex instructional challenges. Through examining the processes and resulting instructional routines of schools and teachers who have delved deeply—in many different ways—into learning about and teaching disciplinary literacy, we hope to shed light on the possible pathways toward learning about and bringing to life disciplinary literacy in middle and high school classrooms.

In chapter 2, we'll turn our attention more specifically to the important role that professional learning structures and routines can play in supporting teacher learning. Together, chapters 1 and 2 set the backdrop for our disciplinary literacy professional learning framework at the heart of this book, introduced in chapter 3.

APPENDIX (Chapter 1)

A Few Notable Resources about Disciplinary Literacy

Resources on Disciplinary Literacy

Buehl, D. *Developing Readers in the Academic Disciplines*. Newark, DE: International Reading Association, 2011.

Draper, R. J., P. Broomhead, A. P. Jensen, J. D. Nokes, and D. Siebert, eds. *(Re)Imagining Content Area Literacy Instruction*. New York: Teachers College Press, 2010.

Jetton, T. L., and C. Shanahan, eds. *Adolescent Literacy in the Academic Disciplines: General Principles and Practical Strategies*. New York: Guilford Press, 2012.

Zwiers, J., and M. Crawford. *Academic Conversations: Classroom Talk That Fosters Critical Thinking and Content Understandings*. Portland, ME: Stenhouse, 2011.

Resources on Science

Cervetti, G., and P. D. Pearson. Reading, Writing, and Thinking Like a Scientist. *Journal of Adolescent and Adult Literacy* 55, no. 7 (2012): 580–586.

Grant, M. C., and D. Fisher. *Reading and Writing in Science: Tools to Develop Disciplinary Literacy*. Thousand Oaks, CA: Corwin, 2009.

Houseal, A., V. Gillis, M. Helmsing, and L. Hutchison. Disciplinary Literacy Through the Lens of the Next Generation Science Standards. *Journal of Adolescent & Adult Literacy* 59, no. 4 (2016): 377–384.

Worth, K., J. Winokur, S. Crissman, and H. Heller-Winokur. *The Essentials of Science and Literacy: A Guide for Teachers*. Portsmouth, NH: Heinemann, 2009.

Resources on Social Studies

Damico, J., M. Baildon, M. Exter, and S. J. Guo. Where We Read from Matters: Disciplinary Literacy in a Ninth-Grade Social Studies Classroom. *Journal of Adolescent & Adult Literacy* 53, no. 4 (2009): 325–335.

Monte-Santo, C., S. De La Paz, and M. Felton. *Reading, Thinking and Writing About History: Teaching Argument Writing to Diverse Learners*. New York: Teachers College, 2014.

Nokes, J. *Building Students' Historical Literacies: Learning to Read and Reason with Historical Texts and Evidence*. New York: Routledge, 2013.

Wineburg, S. *Historical Thinking & Other Unnatural Acts: Charting the Future of Teaching the Past*. Philadelphia: Temple University Press, 2001.

Resources on Math

Adams, A. E., and J. Pegg. Teachers' Enactment of Content Literacy Strategies in Secondary Science and Mathematics Classes. *Journal of Adolescent & Adult Literacy* 56, no. 2 (2012): 151–161.

Burns, M. *Writing in Math Class.* Sausalito, CA: Math Solutions, 2004.

Friedland, E. S., S. E. McMillen, and P. del Prado Hill. Collaborating to Cross the Mathematics-Literacy Divide: An Annotated Bibliography of Literacy Strategies for Mathematics Classrooms. *Journal of Adolescent & Adult Literacy* 55, no. 1 (2011): 57–66.

Resources on English and Language Arts

Cherry-Paul, S., and D. Johansen. *Teaching Interpretation: Using Text Based-Evidence to Construct Meaning.* Portsmouth, NH: Heinemann, 2014.

Smagorinsky, P. Disciplinary Literacy in English Language Arts. *Journal of Adolescent & Adult Literacy* 59, no. 2 (2015): 141–146.

Tarasiuk, T. J. Combining Traditional and Contemporary Texts: Moving My English Class to the Computer Lab. *Journal of Adolescent and Adult Literacy* 53, no. 7 (2010): 543–552.

Resources on Other Content Areas

Wickens, C. M., M. Manderino, J. Parker, and J. Jung. Habits of Practice: Expanding Disciplinary Literacy Frameworks Through a Physical Education Lens. *Journal of Adolescent & Adult Literacy* 59, no. 1 (2015): 75–82.

Wilson, A. A., E. Smith, and D. L. Householder. Using Disciplinary Literacies to Enhance Adolescents' Engineering Design Activity. *Journal of Adolescent & Adult Literacy* 57, no. 8 (2014): 676–686.

CHAPTER 2

Focusing on
Professional Learning

IMPROVING STUDENTS' LITERACY SKILLS in the disciplines will require a great deal of support and new learning experiences for teachers if our goal is to truly support teachers designing and implementing changes in their instructional practices. Unfortunately, most teacher professional learning structures and projects do not situate teachers where they'll be able to make sustained and effective changes to instructional practices.[1] If we are serious about supporting teachers in adopting, adapting, inventing, and teaching disciplinary literacy in their classrooms, then we must pay equal attention to literacy instructional practices *and* teacher professional learning processes.

In this chapter, we ask you to join us in exploring the broad world of teacher professional learning in order to: (1) understand why traditional professional learning experiences have been *ineffective*, (2) synthesize what current research says about *effective* professional learning experiences, and (3) argue that excellent disciplinary literacy teaching and learning are partly the result of excellent professional learning processes. Not all of the research marshaled and discussed here is directly about literacy professional learning; much is not. But, we consider this information to be an important foundation that we have used to develop our multistep framework of professional learning focused on disciplinary literacy. This foundation, along with a focus on specific knowledge about disciplinary literacy, forms the basis of our framework of collaboration for disciplinary literacy professional learning and student achievement.

WHY IS PROFESSIONAL LEARNING IMPORTANT (AND SO OFTEN INEFFECTIVE)?

Although the majority of teachers across levels and content areas nationwide participate in some type of preservice teacher preparation, agreement in the field is that learning to teach is a long process.[2] Moreover, as we discussed in chapter 1, secondary teacher preparation has traditionally focused heavily on content knowledge to the exclusion of other training (particularly the kinds of context-dependent advanced training that might ultimately support adolescents' disciplinary literacy skills). Though novice teachers enter the field with weeks to years of preparation, they have no way to fully master the complex work of teaching before entry. On-the-job professional learning opportunities have always been a mainstay of the profession.

Professional development has a long history in schools. Unfortunately, this history is checkered, at best. Today, most of the professional learning that teachers experience is brief—often in the form of one-day workshops—which leaves teachers with little opportunity to integrate their new learning into their practice, to talk with others about how to apply this new learning, or to review and refine the implementation of newly learned practices over time.[3] The result? This type of professional development, on the whole, has little impact on teachers' practice.[4]

This lack of impact on teaching occurs largely because outsiders to schools (even if they are experts in the field) are unable to personalize their single-session professional development presentations for the various schools and teachers attending their sessions. Alternately, teachers might attend daylong or afternoon workshops within their school districts, which, though slightly more personalized, are again too short to have a lasting impact.

The short-term nature of much professional development means that teachers experience a collection of opportunities to learn new information and practices, yet these opportunities are not coupled with the chance to follow up or process their learning with others over time, resulting in little change in teaching practice. In the case of a challenge such as implementing and scaling disciplinary literacy instruction, the short-term nature and lack of personalization are sure to be unsuccessful, as disciplinary literacy requires specific, context-driven professional learning.

Unfortunately, while the amount and duration of professional learning seem to be quite important, with some suggesting that teachers require at least thirty hours of learning in order to affect practice, simply increasing professional learning time and intensity does not always guarantee a positive change.[5] Many long-term professional learning opportunities can also be ineffective, according to teachers.[6] These opportunities often involve collaboration across time, with teachers working together in teams to make changes, which we applaud. But sometimes these collaborations come with little or no support or guidance. In other cases, teachers might experience long-term professional learning but find that their own knowledge and expertise about their students, classrooms, and schools are rarely, if ever, called upon as the foundation for the development of new practices. Though collaborative learning can be a valuable experience, when teachers work together in teams with little guidance, or when teachers' own ideas are pushed out of the center of such conversations, many report deep dissatisfaction and little learning.[7] These types of long-term learning opportunities can become yet another discrete professional development opportunity that, without proper structures and guidance, results again in little change.

COMBINING PROFESSIONAL LEARNING STRUCTURES TO CREATE AN EFFECTIVE FRAMEWORK

What, then, do teachers need in order to learn in meaningful ways on the job and in ways that will affect and improve their practice? Luckily, research has led to the development of models for this kind of learning. In order to provide teachers with the types of professional learning needed to move their practice forward, they need learning opportunities specific to their school sites and embedded within their jobs.[8] They need learning opportunities that are ongoing and systematic, not merely required weekly meetings, but collaborative times guided by leaders and structures that frame meaningful conversations about practice. Teachers also need opportunities that allow them to tailor what they learn to the specific students in their classrooms. And they need time and space to reflect on their learning, particularly with colleagues with whom they can give and receive just-in-time feedback.[9] Unfortunately, many professional learning initiatives lose steam or fail, in part because they focus on only one of these key aspects. Or, they invest in only one key structural mechanism such as a literacy coach, without simultaneously designing collaborative learning times or other structures that would support the coaching work.

The trick, of course, is that if we know which conditions lead to successful teacher professional learning and changes in practice, how can we design professional learning projects and structures that have just enough of the necessary ingredients, while still respecting the limited time and funds available in schools? In other words, what is the right balance between what works and what is feasible? More specifically, for this book, which models best provide secondary teachers with what they need in order to be effective teachers of disciplinary literacy as a component of their content-area instruction?

Our work with teachers has led to the development of a flexible framework that hits on all of the key components mentioned, while focusing on disciplinary literacy learning, specifically as an area that requires deep collaborative work across time in order to see lasting change. This framework is blended, instead of investing solely in one professional learning structure (such as professional learning communities). As we describe in chapter 3, it builds on three powerful professional learning structures that together support adult learning and instructional change (see figure 2.1). This framework is designed such that project designers can take the flexible structures and combine them uniquely in order to best fit their contexts.

FIGURE 2.1 Three flexible professional learning structures

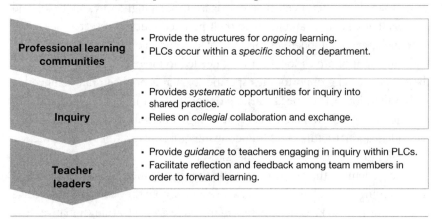

In disciplinary literacy professional learning projects, we have identified and invested in three key professional learning structures: disciplinary literacy–focused professional learning communities (PLCs), inquiry as a means of learning and reflecting within PLCs, and teacher leaders to guide and facilitate inquiry work within PLCs. We have chosen these because they support teachers from a wide array of content areas to build an understanding of implementing disciplinary literacy across time. Together, these three structures form the backbone of our multistep professional learning framework and can be tailored to specific school contexts and needs. Though there are other finer-grained aspects of our framework, such as key opportunities to learn from experts (which are explored in chapter 3 and beyond), we turn our attention here to the three professional learning structures, a rationale for why these approaches are effective, and an initial explanation of how these structures support each other.

Professional learning communities

Over the past decade or so, PLCs have become almost ubiquitous in schools. The result of their widespread adoption is that schools have interpreted the model broadly and have enacted PLCs in ways that deviate greatly from the intention behind the model. Though PLCs now come in all shapes and sizes, they have traditionally been built around a handful of powerful ideas: a focus on student and adult learning; establishing and maintaining a culture of collaboration; a focus on results (in the form of improved teaching and learning); a focus on individual as well as collective learning and inquiry; and a focus on continuous improvement.[10]

While creating structures that bring teachers together regularly is not hard, creating a culture that embraces those structures as well as a common vision (like disciplinary literacy) to drive the work of teachers within those structures can prove much more difficult.[11] Getting folks into the same room together at the same time every week can be easy enough, but creating the conditions for collective learning and inquiry or a focus on continuous improvement is no simple feat. A recent report on teachers' experiences with professional development found that teachers were less satisfied with their PLCs than any other professional learning opportunity.[12] This dissatisfaction was likely due to the types of mandates that Joan Talbert found teachers often experienced within PLCs, in which a model intended to generate organic opportunities for teacher learning and inquiry instead was filled with compliance-oriented and test-focused conversations.[13]

Ideally, PLCs emerge from needs identified within a school community and provide a venue for regular conversations among various stakeholders, focused on improving aspects of instructional practice.[14] In reality, however, the creation of effective PLCs is a complex endeavor, and many groups of teachers working together struggle to find a shared vision or approach to their work. Too often, school and district leaders create teams with the assumption that groups of teachers will know how to work together effectively and that this work will result in improved outcomes for students. Yet, without ongoing structure and guidance, this is rarely the case.[15]

While PLCs have been conceptualized and enacted in a variety of ways, we use what Nancy Fichtman Dana and Diane Yendol-Hoppey characterize as the work of PLCs: groups that come together regularly to engage in collaborative inquiry into teaching and learning activities.[16] These authors provide a list of ten key elements that characterize a healthy PLC, many of which overlap with those previously mentioned. This useful list suggests that "healthy PLCs. . . .

- establish and maintain a vision of the work
- build trust among group members
- pay attention to the ways power can influence group dynamics
- understand and embrace collaboration
- encourage, recognize, and appreciate diversity within the group
- promote the development of critical friends
- hold the group accountable for and document their learning
- understand change and acknowledge the discomfort it may bring to some PLC members
- have a comprehensive view of what constitutes data, and are willing to consider all forms and types of data throughout their PLC work
- work with their building administrators"[17]

While several of these tenets are foundational across common conceptualizations of PLCs (e.g., embracing collaboration, crafting and sharing a vision, building trust, etc.), others are more specific to Dana and Yendol-Hoppey's vision of PLC enactment (e.g., development of "critical friends" and paying attention to power dynamics).[18]

We embrace this particular vision of PLCs because it places less emphasis on student achievement and more on the facilitative moves that support adult learning and group collaboration. We think that this collaboration-focused approach is key to seeing change in instruction when the work is as complex as adopting a disciplinary literacy stance. While the classic notion that PLCs should focus on student learning and achievement is partially helpful, we find Dana and Yendol-Hoppey's explicit attention to working with administrators, paying attention to power dynamics, and embracing the discomfort that comes with change useful for those who are convening and supporting PLCs. It is an important reminder to attend to the particular dynamics that allow for adult learning.

Collaborative inquiry

PLCs provide a useful and regular structure in which professional learning can take place. But, while teachers have spent years learning how to teach students effectively, they have not necessarily learned how to work effectively with each other or how best to learn together, even though working together will allow them to better solve their instructional dilemmas. Adopting an inquiry stance, as a focus of this collective work, can provide a much-needed structure to help guide teachers when they are working together in disciplinary literacy PLCs. Simply put, a focus on inquiry means teachers bring questions to the table to puzzle through together. These could be questions that emerge organically or questions in response to guidance from administrators or teacher leaders. Or they could be questions that arise in the context of protocols used to guide shared conversations about practice. The following are a few examples of inquiries about disciplinary literacy on which teachers might collaborate to find new instructional approaches:

- A math teacher notices that students who previously excelled with calculations struggle to extract information from data presented to them in the form of tables and diagrams. She asks her PLC to help her figure out how to approach this instructional challenge.
- An administrator suggests that a team of history teachers create a scope and sequence related to the disciplinary literacy skills they will teach across grade levels in a high school. The team comes together to discuss the questions: "What are the disciplinary literacy skills we already teach to our

students? What do we think they need? When and how should we best teach those skills across students' high school history experiences?"

- A team of English teachers gathers regularly to discuss curricula and how to incorporate disciplinary literacy more explicitly into their practice. The team often uses protocols to guide their discussion. Using the Consultancy Protocol (available on the School Reform Initiative website, http://school reforminitiative.org), which asks the presenting teacher to share a problem of practice to guide conversation, one team member asked her group to focus on the following dilemma: "I have been working on teaching my students to link evidence to their arguments in literary analytical writing, but I'm finding that more than half of them are still struggling with more basic reading and comprehension. How can I balance the need to shore up those foundational skills and work on developing disciplinary literacy skills at the same time?"

Inquiry, as used here, is premised on the idea that, working together around problems of practice, teachers can generate knowledge, ideas, and practices that will lead to positive change in teaching and learning.[19] This collaboration leads to more idea and practice generation than individual teachers might achieve alone. Teacher inquiry, as with PLCs, also helps to push back on the often-isolated nature of the teaching profession and to create spaces where uncertainty and trial and error are valued and even sought out as teachers work together to develop new understandings and practices. Recent research has found that professional learning that includes teachers working together over extended periods of time around shared problems of practice is more likely to lead to meaningful changes in practice than single-session, one-stop professional development workshops.[20] This sort of meaningful change is needed in the case of improving disciplinary literacy instruction in a school.

Inquiry, though, is not automatic when teachers come together. Teachers, over the course of a typical day, love to engage in casual conversation about the profession, sharing information about students, bemoaning new state-mandated tests, or chatting about life beyond school. The teaching profession has historically honored teachers' privacy and autonomy, so teachers working together need support to push beyond these norms.[21] Tamara Holmlund Nelson et al. describe the "congenial conversations" that many teams of teachers engage in that focus on preserving safety and privacy and the need to move toward

"collegial conversations," where teachers dig into practice and build new knowledge together.[22] To achieve these conversations, PLC-based inquiry requires
structure that pushes teachers into deeper, messier conversations. Often this
structure comes in the form of inquiry cycles, which follow a set yet flexible routine over the course of weeks or even months (see figure 2.2 for typical inquiry
cycle steps):

1. Team members examine student data or frame a shared question of practice.
2. Team members generate ideas to address the question or problem of practice that emerged from the examination of data or that team members
   framed together.
3. Individuals try out these newly generated ideas individually and then return
   to the group to discuss findings and how things went.
4. Together, group members reflect on the changes they made to practice
   and how well those changes addressed their question or helped to provide
   insight into the problem of practice.

FIGURE 2.2   **Typical inquiry cycle steps**

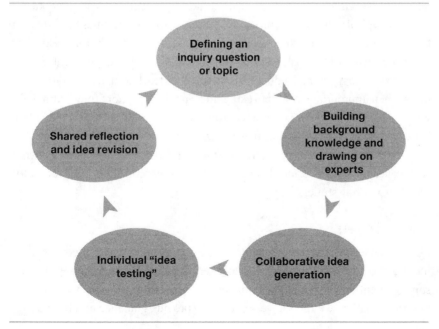

5. In many cases, this leads to the generation of new questions or problems of practice, which team members then inquire into in a similar, systematic fashion.

For example, an interdisciplinary team of teachers might come together because students do not seem to be fully engaging with new material as deeply as they might, being mostly passive as new material is introduced. Therefore, the team might decide to conduct an inquiry cycle about classroom discussion, with the goal of encouraging students to more fully express their own ideas to each other, to better engage with new material. The team may read lots of research and practice-focused advice about implementing discussions across their class-rooms in different disciplines, and each teacher might choose one or two new instructional practices to implement in class. The team then comes together to watch video footage of the students' discussions and provide feedback to each other about how well the practice seems to be working. The team might feel that the new practices around discussion are helping students engage, but they also might notice in their collaborative conversations that students are not often using discipline-specific vocabulary as they talk. So, the team decides to move on to a new inquiry cycle about how to improve students' productive vocabulary skills.

This type of inquiry cycle provides teachers with opportunities to learn from their own practice, with embedded opportunities for feedback from peers. For example, a team of Spanish teachers might help a member explore patterns of using text in class, giving feedback to support that teacher in incorporating text more when appropriate to support students' Spanish use more fully. Ultimately, when ideas for new practices emerge from these inquiries, there is a direct link between teachers' practice and these new ideas, increasing the likelihood that teachers will see value in the learning emerging from their collaborative work with colleagues. As a result, this new learning is more likely to take root, ulti-mately benefiting student learning.

Teacher leaders

PLCs provide an effective structure for regularly bringing teachers together. Inquiry provides a frame for what teachers do within those PLCs–providing some content and shape to their conversations. By introducing teacher leaders into the equation, we then have someone to provide guidance and boundaries to this structure and content in order for teachers to be most effective in their work together.

Teacher leadership is not a new concept in the profession. Historically, teacher leaders had formal roles to provide various types of guidance and support to others, such as the department head at a high school. More recently, teacher leaders have begun to play roles that allow them to provide mentorship or coaching to peers, or to provide particular curricular expertise, such as with a new math curriculum.[23] Alternately, some teacher leaders foster conversations among peers about curriculum and instruction.[24] Though privacy has been the norm within the teaching profession for years, many have documented a new willingness among teachers to work collaboratively.[25] This move toward more willing collaboration means that teacher leaders have new potential to guide generative conversations within teams, which can result in meaningful ideas for new instructional practices and ultimately deeper student learning.

Scholars of teacher leadership have theorized that such leadership has come into the profession in distinct waves.[26] In the current wave, teacher leaders are seen as key levers in shifting school culture in order to have an impact on teaching and learning. PLCs, focused on teacher inquiry–into how best to integrate disciplinary literacy in content-area instruction or other complex problems of practice–provide an opportunity for teacher leaders to guide just the type of cultural change that these authors point to. Thus, guided inquiry, within the structure of PLCs and led by teacher leaders, seems to combine the key ingredients needed for instructional improvement.[27] And, when necessary, teacher leaders can also bring in external expertise–in the form of outsiders to consult or readings to digest and process collectively–to further build capacity among PLC members by providing content to guide inquiry and experimentation.

HOW DO PLCS, INQUIRY, AND TEACHER LEADERSHIP COMPLEMENT EACH OTHER

Alone, PLCs, teacher inquiry, or teacher leadership do not hold the same potential for creating change–and particularly change around disciplinary literacy instructional practices–that these elements hold when working together. As detailed above, PLCs are structural in nature and can provide the boundaries and routines needed to bring teachers together to make change. Inquiry can provide the guidance for conversations over time so that teachers can decide together what to discuss and how to reflect on changes in practice that they try out in their individual classrooms. And teacher leaders can help teams of teachers decide on which inquiries are best to guide their instructional experiments, to help them reflect together, and to then decide on next steps, both individually and collectively.

Working together, these three professional learning structures contribute to the type of in-depth professional learning that experts have said are necessary for effective changes in practice to emerge and be sustained. In our own work, we have found that the shift to disciplinary literacy instruction is a complex challenge that relies on teachers to generate new instructional practices, and therefore, it is a subject that carries a need for deep and lasting professional learning. In our experience, the unique combination of these three structures breeds success among groups working together on disciplinary literacy professional learning.

In the chapters that follow, we turn to the specifics of how these three professional learning structures—PLCs, inquiry, and teacher leadership—work in tandem with other key design elements to create an effective multistep framework for professional learning for secondary teachers focused on disciplinary literacy. This collaborative framework allows teachers to generate new practices that ultimately lead to the integration of disciplinary literacy practices into content-area instruction across the secondary curriculum, thereby improving student achievement and engagement in disciplinary content.

CHAPTER 3

A New Model for Disciplinary Literacy Professional Learning

WE NOW TURN our attention to creating spaces in schools where collaborative inquiry into disciplinary literacy instruction can take place. This is no small task. Many schools and districts struggle to design professional learning that leads to meaningful and lasting improvement. Creating a professional learning project that will address disciplinary literacy requires careful planning, thoughtful and iterative implementation, and clear evaluation. This chapter takes what we know about disciplinary literacy, what we know about professional learning, and what we have learned from schools and districts we have worked with to posit a new multistep framework to guide professional learning for improving disciplinary literacy.

We have come to this framework after school leaders have repeatedly asked us to design professional learning about disciplinary literacy for teachers in a variety of settings. Because of what we know about the need for context-specific and ongoing professional learning, we found ourselves frequently helping school leaders to design initiatives that could work for their specific contexts. We found this design and implementation work to be different from place to place, but the overarching structure had several shared components. This evolved into our seven-step framework for designing and implementing disciplinary literacy professional learning that results in instructional change.

Our seven-step framework for designing and implementing collaborative disciplinary literacy professional learning is guided by four key habits of working that set the stage for an action space for improvement. We begin by describing what an *action space* is and how to open one with the potential for improvement and lasting change. Then we explore the four key habits of working and how they contribute to the opening of action spaces. Finally, we outline our seven-step process for establishing and supporting disciplinary literacy professional learning projects–the main focus of this book.

CREATING ACTION SPACES: THE HOW AND WHY

Professional learning projects are often short-lived and frequently fail to attend to the particulars of individual school contexts. Most often, if these projects and initiatives do not quickly lead to transformations of instructional practice and improvements in student achievement, then they are viewed as ineffective or even as failures.[1] But some, including us, take a slightly different view of school reform projects. We rely on the theory of action spaces to explain this broader view of school reform work, because this theory acknowledges the sometimes short duration of professional learning as well as the way that professional learning shifts across collaborative projects.

Joseph McDonald articulates a theory about action spaces to describe when and how circumstances can converge in a school context to create conditions for improvement.[2] McDonald writes: "[A]ction space is exceptional space. Although it pops up from time to time nearly everywhere, it is not ordinary work space. It is endowed with extraordinary resources pulled together by luck and pluck. These provide the margin that makes reform conceivable. Action space disturbs the equilibrium of schooling-as-usual in a way that policy and professional education cannot manage to do."[3] This theory takes as a given that action spaces– opportunities for generative work and change–open and inevitably close, and that schools can use resources wisely to create conditions that can open an action space and spur improvement.

As we work with schools trying to begin disciplinary literacy initiatives, we use this action space idea and the resources that create an action space to help schools assess their own readiness for change. We discuss this key notion when working with disciplinary literacy leadership teams to help them make early decisions about the type and timing of professional learning experiences they would like to design and implement. We find the action space idea critical in helping leadership teams break free from more traditional (and less effective) notions of professional learning as temporary, succeed-or-fail endeavors that make little lasting difference in schools.

To create an action space, three resources have to be created and/or to coalesce: money, civic capacity, and professional capacity. Each of the three resources is important in how it contributes to school change:

- **Money.** This resource is somewhat self-explanatory. It's the capital a school is able to marshal to support a reform initiative and its operation over time. Most effective professional learning projects involve time for collaboration, and there are many ways in which money can be used to purchase time and other important project supports.
- **Civic capacity.** This resource has to do with the broader school community. McDonald describes it as "the extent to which various sectors of the community understand, support, and actively contribute to reform."[4] This does not mean that all community members necessarily work on the initiative in similar ways or even participate at all, but that various individuals throughout the community, including leaders, support the work and goals of the project.
- **Professional capacity.** This final resource has to do with the capacity to do and sustain the work of the project, and it can include many facets. McDonald describes this as the "distributed intellectual, technical, and organizational know-how" an organization can marshal to support the project.[5] This capacity can be changed by a variety of factors including how much other professional learning work teachers are being asked to do in the same time frame as the project. Teachers' readiness for the work of the project also affects this capacity. Taking on learning that asks teachers to move practice too far from existing instructional approaches often extends beyond the professional capacity both of schools and teams.

According to McDonald's action space theory, a combination of these three resources is necessary to begin and sustain a school improvement initiative. If one of the resources disappears, then the action space will collapse with it. If a school wants to create a successful disciplinary literacy project, then it must consider the sustainability of these three resource strands and plan accordingly, even for a project's end.

Describing action spaces this way may seem dramatic. When an action space comes to an abrupt end, it can feel like failure. However, McDonald disagrees, saying that the eventual collapse of all action spaces is just part of the process of school reform. It is natural and inevitable; therefore, project design teams should plan for endings as well as beginnings. McDonald says action spaces that lead to effective professional learning also lead to increased professional capacity, a capacity that remains even when a particular project ends. We agree. Increased professional capacities are beneficial for a school, despite the fact that each particular project invariably ends. We think that schools can carefully plan to manage the resources available to ensure maximum and lasting improvement across a disciplinary literacy professional learning initiative. Our seven-step framework for planning and implementing a disciplinary learning initiative takes this action space theory into account. Furthermore, the planning phase of our framework pushes design teams to maximize their resources to create an action space for disciplinary literacy improvement and to build capacity such that new practices last beyond the closing of the action space connected to the initiative.

KEY WORKING HABITS OF AN ACTION SPACE FOR DISCIPLINARY LEARNING IMPROVEMENT

In our work with schools and districts, we've come to believe that the idea of an action space is uniquely fitted for the complex work of disciplinary literacy professional learning. In order for this action space to be fruitful, we have developed four key habits of working that create a culture of learning for this type of professional learning initiative. In disciplinary literacy, we often talk about the habits of mind we want students to adopt, the habits that mark ways of thinking and knowing within particular disciplines. Here we talk about working habits for the teacher professional learning communities we seek to build—communities focused on improving disciplinary literacy instruction. Projects that adopt these habits over time see greater instructional improvement and higher teacher engagement. We describe each of the four key habits briefly here.

Working habit #1: *Balancing content and process*

We talked in chapter 2 about collaboration as a key aspect of any professional learning initiative that leads to meaningful change. In a disciplinary literacy initiative, collaboration is certainly a key to success. But how teams of practitioners learn to learn together and manage their time in this type of initiative must balance with a focus on the content of disciplinary literacy practices. In other words, teams of teachers must not lose too much time or focus on either process or product, instead finding a happy medium between these twin goals. This simultaneous focus on process and content is a key to success, because it equips teams with the knowledge they need to do the work and the collaborative capacity to effect change as groups, rather than individuals.

Schools, especially at the secondary level, have traditionally had cultures that lend themselves toward isolation and autonomy.[6] Teachers have historically spent much time with students and less time with each other. But in order to change literacy practices across classrooms, grade levels, and departments, teachers need to work together. This collaboration is important, but just because it is important does not mean that teachers have had the necessary experience to collaborate effectively right away.

Too often, professional learning initiatives solely focus on the *content* of interest—in our case, disciplinary literacy—with the hope that maximizing time spent on the content will result in steep improvements in instruction. But this does not hold true for our work with schools and districts. Our experience has shown that teacher teams, even those with experience collaborating and especially those without, need to learn to work together as groups in ways that are structured to keep participants engaged and maintain the momentum of the work. By focusing on collaborative processes up front and throughout the project, teams are building their capacity to effectively and collectively build new knowledge about disciplinary literacy and then to implement those ideas in content classes.

A focus on process translates into a few actionable steps: team building early in the work; exploration of protocols and structured-conversation tools; goal setting for each inquiry cycle; and, over time, making practice visible through teachers' visits to each other's classrooms, collaborative analysis of student work, and other types of group reflection. By setting norms for discussion early on and using protocols and structured conversations throughout, teams of teachers can avoid some of the typical traps of group conversations. Without these safeguards, groups often get carried away on tangents or fail to do any sort of action planning by a conversation's end. If groups do not feel as though they are making progress over the course of their meetings together or that things are moving too quickly, members can disengage from the work. A clear focus on process can help leaders and team members manage their time effectively and eventually work together toward goals they determine for themselves. In particular, an up-front investment in group process pays big dividends in disciplinary literacy content learning down the line.

The focus on process is only a piece of the work though, and the focus on content is also an important component of any disciplinary literacy project. As teams of teachers explore various facets of disciplinary literacy instruction (e.g., academic vocabulary or writing in a particular discipline), they need a focus on content to support their learning. This means they will need access to research and tools written for practitioners in order to explore options, learn from the research and experiences of others, and ultimately decide which practices they will focus on in their inquiry. Coaches, instructional leaders, team leaders, or outside consultants can provide this access; in our experience, a combination of the personnel involved in a project provides it. This balance between content and process is the first and most important habit of working that marks a successful disciplinary literacy action space.

Working habit #2: *Creating a culture of adaptation and invention*

The second key working habit for a disciplinary literacy professional learning project is to create a culture of adaptation and invention. Professional learning projects are sometimes characterized by a culture wherein no one is accountable for change, and new learning is soon forgotten. Others are characterized by forced implementation, wherein teachers must immediately try particular newly learned instructional practices or curricula. If we are to change instruction to support stronger literacy practices, we have to create professional learning projects where the culture is not so permissive as to be ineffective and not so authoritarian as to inspire resentment among participants. This balance is not easy to strike, but we think creating a culture that values innovation is a good way to gain instructional traction.

There are several reasons why a culture of invention and adaptation is a key to success in this sort of initiative. First, disciplinary literacy is a relatively new idea, and in many content areas, extensive information about how to best provide content-specific literacy instruction is unavailable. In these domains, where less is known about disciplinary literacy, teachers themselves, with their attendant expertise, are perfectly positioned (with proper support) to invent new practices. In other content areas where more research has been done and more instruction designed to support students, teachers—with their specific knowledge of students and school context—are best positioned to adopt and adapt existing work. No matter the level of research and information that exists, teachers are still responsible for matching these practices to particular students or incorporating them into existing curricula. In disciplinary literacy professional learning projects, the teachers themselves are the main agents of discovery, invention, and change, and this work requires a supportive culture that embraces and celebrates experimentation.

Second, a culture of adaptation and invention is often engaging because it situates teachers as action researchers who investigate the rationale for and effectiveness of new practices in their own highly particular contexts. This sense of autonomy empowers teachers with the time and space to find creative ways to marry content being studied with particular literacy practices. It is a key to raising student skills. And because each group of students has a unique combination of needs, teachers need the support and encouragement from initiatives like these to make their own decisions about implementation to meet those needs. Teachers in secondary classrooms are typically trained to be experts in their disciplinary domains, and when initiatives do not ask teachers to be inventive, we miss important opportunities to capitalize on the immense expertise that teachers already possess. Finally, a culture of adaptation and invention generates enthusiasm among participants, which in turn leads to a stronger platform from which to spread the learning of participants to others in the school.

A disciplinary literacy professional learning initiative must take all this into account if it is to create meaningful change. By encouraging teacher participants to explore and tinker early in an initiative, rather than immediately deliver revised curricula or higher student achievement, we see teachers taking what is known broadly about strong literacy instruction and adapting it to support their disciplinary work and creating new cultures in their classrooms and broader departments. This spirit of experimentation also embraces failure, allowing teachers to come back to the table with ideas that have not been successful and, collectively, to reshape and retool in order to return to their classrooms with newly envisioned practices. Inside a culture that embraces the messiness of the change process, we have seen teacher teams approach their work with focused curiosity and joyful inventiveness as they work collaboratively to improve disciplinary achievement for all students regardless of skills or background.

Working habit #3: *Attending equally to intermediate and disciplinary literacy skills*

We have discussed in earlier chapters the Shanahans' framework (see figure 1.1) for increased literacy specialization, and we've talked extensively about the importance of disciplinary literacy for improving adolescent achievement in secondary schools.[7] We do not mean to suggest though, in emphasizing the importance of disciplinary literacy, that we downplay the value and need to also think about intermediate literacy skills in secondary classrooms, especially in cases where students might be lagging in grade-level work.

Our work with secondary teachers and students has repeatedly demonstrated that intermediate skills are often a necessary focal point for instruction in a variety of disciplines.[8] You may remember from chapter 1 that we discussed intermediate strategies, which used to be called content-area reading strategies, and that teachers sometimes resisted the widespread incorporation of these strategies in their classrooms. But our experience in collaborative projects around disciplinary literacy tells a somewhat different story that pushes us to include this as one of the essential habits for these types of initiatives.

Our work has shown us that when teachers collaborate to uncover what their students know and need to know, to explore priorities related to initiating novices into their disciplines, and to discover new instructional practices for their classrooms, those teachers often find that students need to shore up intermediate skills in comprehension and fluency. We find again and again that teachers are happy to learn about and provide this instruction when needed, when they see their own students requiring specific intermediate skill work. Teachers in disciplinary literacy professional learning projects often focus on particular inquiry questions over time—for example, a math team deciding to focus on pushing students to discuss their reasoning and problem solving together. Then, over the course of the inquiry, teams may find that some skills that are not discipline specific are influencing how students perform with the new disciplinary literacy instruction provided. The math team just mentioned found that students were discussing their reasoning together, but they were not using math-specific or general academic vocabulary as effectively as they might. So the team decided to focus on several more intermediate vocabulary routines: encouraging students to use academic vocabulary aloud more frequently, introducing word walls and word journals, and instigating for word use as a matter of habit in the classroom.

This sort of trajectory is one we have seen frequently with teams focusing collaboratively on disciplinary literacy. The demands of high levels of disciplinary literacy instruction often require that teachers be able to effectively determine what students know and need to know, and then to provide intermediate-level instruction as needed to shore up foundational skills, all while still driving a disciplinary literacy agenda forward. We often describe this as a complex dance between intermediate and disciplinary foci over time, to ensure that students have all the tools they need to be inducted into novice disciplinary communities. When teachers experience this intermediate instruction as supportive of their bigger and more content-specific classroom goals, we often see exciting new ideas for intermediate instruction, too, as this dual intermediate and disciplinary focus becomes a natural focus for teams.

Working habit #4: *Positioning teachers as learners within projects*

The last important habit of working that we believe contributes to productive action spaces in disciplinary literacy initiatives has to do with how teachers and other participants are positioned. Teachers in professional learning projects are often positioned either as empty receptacles that must take new information and implement it, or as experts who are supposed to know how to handle every challenge. In our experience, this opens up very little space for adaptation, invention, and productive failure to take shape. Instead, we encourage a habit of positioning teachers as active learners in a project, co-constructors of the new practices that will result from collaborative inquiry.

This positioning of participants as learners, including those who choose to take on leadership roles, creates space for teachers to tinker and experiment with new practices in the interest of finding tools that work for their particular context and students. By encouraging participants to approach their work this way, we find that teachers feel less paralyzed by the pressure to raise achievement instantly. They feel less pressure to find the best possible practices at every stage of the inquiry process. Of course, we want strong practices and greater achievement to emerge ultimately. However, because there is still much to uncover, invent, and adapt in the process of determining best disciplinary literacy instructional practices, teachers need to feel free to take what they know, combined with what they are learning in the project, to gradually invent and experiment with new routines. Sometimes teachers in professional learning settings can feel frustrated if they attempt new practices and do not see results quickly. This can be discouraging and lead teachers to quickly revert to business as usual. But when a discourse about experimentation and learning is encouraged, a space opens up to discuss what happens when things do not immediately work as expected. We learn to collaboratively tweak practices or try others in order to achieve results.

Leaders of teacher teams learning in front of the team members they work with provide modeling of the risks and vulnerabilities that come with making instructional practice public. By showing that they want to present their own dilemmas of practice for discussion, team leaders show that everyone is learning and that the process of collaboration can lead to important improvements. This learning process and culture of experimentation has to be embedded at all levels of a successful project, from the design team to teacher leaders to team participants.

The reliance on learning as a core value can present challenges, though, as sometimes participants have to embrace uncertainty. We often remind teacher participants in these initiatives that the body of research in literacy can only get us so far in determining which instructional practices are going to be most effective for particular groups of students. The research gives us strong consensus in some areas and practically radio silence in others, so teachers need to help fill in some of those gaps. Sometimes participants are disconcerted by the uncertainty in the process, but over time, many come to feel as though it frees them to make decisions for themselves. As this way of working becomes a habit, we see teams embracing uncertainty as they rely more on their own innovations to craft appropriate instructional practices for their own students.

Together, these four habits of working characterize the most effective action spaces we have been fortunate to be part of, and they continually renew the enthusiasm and engagement of the participants who are working hard on disciplinary literacy questions. But in order to open one of these action spaces, careful and thoughtful work must take place. We now introduce the seven-step framework we have found to be effective at opening and sustaining action spaces to improve disciplinary literacy and create meaningful and lasting professional learning.

SEVEN-STEP FRAMEWORK FOR INITIATING AND SUSTAINING A DISCIPLINARY LITERACY PROFESSIONAL LEARNING INITIATIVE

In our ongoing work with schools and teachers, we have always focused on three phases of development: planning, implementation, and expansion/evaluation.

Over time, we have uncovered key steps within each of these broad phases to support the creation of action spaces with the most potential for change (see figure 3.1). We briefly introduce each of these phases and the specific steps within them, and then unpack each in subsequent chapters, illustrated with snapshots from disciplinary literacy projects from schools and districts that have done this work.

Important steps in the planning phase

In the planning phase of the process, before a professional learning project begins, there are two steps to follow in order to ensure that the resulting initiative is as robust as possible:

1. **Forming a literacy leadership and design team and identifying readiness for change (chapter 4).** Not all sites are well suited at every moment to take on a complex, collaborative learning project. By forming a literacy leadership and design team, and reviewing a school's or district's current strategic

FIGURE 3.1   The seven-step framework for designing and implementing disciplinary literacy professional learning projects

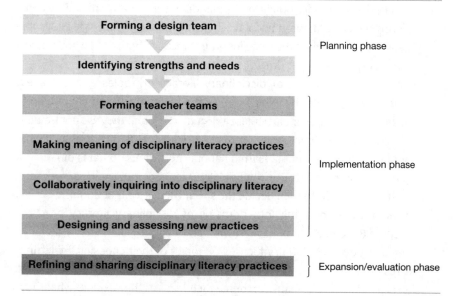

plans for improvement, a school can best determine the ideal time to begin a project like this and to marshal civic capacity for the project.

2. **Assessing needs and identifying levers for change (chapter 5).** Schools planning to implement a project like this benefit from going through a reflective process in which they consider several factors: the general strengths and needs of students; the strengths and needs of teachers; the available organizational structures such as shared planning time; and organizational opportunities like local funders or support personnel like coaches. Each of these elements may support the opening of an action space.

Important steps in the implementation phase

Following the planning phase, there are several key components to successful implementation once an action space has been opened. These steps help support participants' development of new collaborative ways of working together and introduce them to the big ideas in the field of disciplinary literacy. If done well, the implementation steps create an environment in which a particular action space can remain open for the duration of the initiative:

3. **Forming teams of content and/or cross-content area teachers and leaders (chapter 6).** A huge component of a successful initiative over time has to do with the smart and thoughtful formation of collaborative teams. By considering which configurations of teachers might have the most leverage for change together, we set the stage for groups that can both design and implement new practices over time.

4. **Making initial meaning of disciplinary literacy principles and practices (chapter 7).** Despite the extensive training many secondary content-area teachers receive in their particular subject matter, often they are not trained in literacy or disciplinary literacy in particular. This means that teams should explore some initial learning about the various domains of literacy up front in order to identify potential areas for later inquiry. This work sets the stage for teams to then decide the specific focus for their inquiries.

5. **Collaboratively inquiring into domains of disciplinary literacy practice (chapter 8).** Once teams have formed and explored domains of literacy, they begin cycles of inquiry focused on topics of their choosing. By letting teams prioritize where they would like to begin and how they would like to focus their attention, teams can refine their ideas as they explore what they

know about a topic and how they might start to adapt instructional practices to best serve students.

6. **Designing, testing, and assessing new disciplinary literacy practices (chapter 9).** As teams work within their inquiry domains, they begin to design new practices and implement them. After implementation begins the work of collecting student data to discern the efficacy of new practices and to assess whether they should be continued and spread to other classrooms. Often the work of this step also involves considering what doesn't work about particular practices and whether other literacy domains are interfering with success. Sometimes this work involves a decision about when to end a particular inquiry cycle or when to stick with the same domain for a while longer.

Important steps in the expansion/evaluation phase

In a given initiative, teachers may cycle through the implementation steps multiple times as they explore a variety of topics and domains. But, at a certain point in their learning, teams begin to consider whether and how they should share their learning and new practices with those not in the project. This work often includes attempts to scale new practices across grade levels and departments and, necessarily, requires some new collaborative strategies and leads to the final step in the process:

7. **Refining and sharing new disciplinary literacy practices within and across content areas (chapter 10).** As instructional practices become more refined, teacher teams will invariably begin to consider when and how to share their practices with others outside their teams. Though sharing among teachers can be countercultural, sharing disciplinary literacy practices is an important key to schoolwide growth in literacy, and so supporting teams as they begin to share is critical to spreading the positive effects of the project to the broader school community.

In part II, we detail the seven steps of our framework and provide our best lessons for how schools might undertake this process for a project that is well designed and uniquely suited to their particular contexts and students. As we reiterate in several places, these steps are meant to be suggestive instead of prescriptive. Ultimately, each school and leadership team will chart its own course. We believe that considering and progressing through these seven steps of work can provide fodder for planning and reflection along the way.

Designing
and Enacting
Disciplinary Literacy
Professional Learning

CHAPTER 4

Forming a Leadership Team and Identifying Readiness for Change

STARTING A DISCIPLINARY LITERACY PROFESSIONAL LEARNING INITIATIVE

If you have worked in a school for any amount of time, then you have likely seen the way that most professional learning initiatives begin. A school- or district-based leader attends a conference or pores over student achievement scores, identifies a targeted need, hires a consultant or purchases an instructional program to solve the identified problem, and then enlists every teacher in the school to attend related professional development workshops or prescribed professional learning community (PLC) meetings. Sound familiar? If you've lived through this sequence of events, then you likely also know that this process rarely solves the original identified problem, at least not in a systemic, sustained manner.

This all-too-common sequence of events is part of what has recently been termed the "Common Theory of School Change."[1] This common theory is nearly universally held and accepted. If you listen closely to the rhetoric of politicians, policy makers, and school leaders, you'll hear the same song: all we need to fix any educational problem is the right professional development package or a new set of research-based instructional strategies. Of course, this common theory assumes that the right answer to most educational dilemmas is well known, and that the solution lies simply in getting faculty to implement that solution. This is what Ron Heifetz, Alexander Grashow, and Marty Linsky would call a "technical" view of educational dilemmas, reflecting the notion that most dilemmas have ready-made, known solutions.[2] All we need to do is implement the solution. This kind of thinking has ushered in wave after wave of solutions that are sold to schools and teachers in various packages: sustained silent reading, scripted curricula, close reading, and so on.

While the common theory may be useful for helping schools make small, surface-level changes–tinkering at the edges of instructional improvement–this series of events is fairly useless at promoting deep, sustainable change in which teachers shift the ways they think about and teach their content. Perhaps you've guessed by now that this is certainly the case with disciplinary literacy. When considering a shift toward teaching disciplinary literacy, there are few shortcuts, prepackaged curricula, or known solutions. Disciplinary literacy work requires invention, adaptation, and a great deal of adult professional learning. Programs, consultants, or packages that claim otherwise are best treated with caution. Let's focus here on step one of our seven-step framework as we explore forming a leadership team to begin planning an initiative.

A DIFFERENT APPROACH TO PLANNING A DISCIPLINARY LITERACY PROFESSIONAL LEARNING INITIATIVE

For most middle and high school teachers nationwide, adopting a disciplinary literacy stance toward teaching content represents a fundamental shift in the way they think and teach. Moreover, adopting a disciplinary literacy stance is an adaptive (rather than technical) endeavor.[3] In other words, when entering into disciplinary literacy work, middle and high school teachers must be prepared to *invent* and *adapt* as opposed to merely *adopt*, and they must purposefully foster this stance in a project.[4] With research about the effects of specific disciplinary literacy practices constantly emerging, any new initiative in this domain must be approached with the understanding that teachers are active learners, designers, and inventors who can take that new research and build upon it to develop and enact new practices. This is a far cry from the passive professional learning suggested by the common theory, and we combat this theory with the structures to support ongoing learning: PLCs, collaborative inquiry, and teacher leadership. Disciplinary literacy professional learning places educators in an adaptive space, where they must collaboratively inquire into their own work habits and assumptions, and design new strategies based on evidence from their own classroom experiments.

If schools move away from the common theory approach and instead use and adapt the seven-step framework we lay out in this book, then they must begin by engaging in a thoughtful planning process. Much of the early planning of a disciplinary literacy professional learning initiative consists of building a disciplinary literacy leadership team and determining school readiness, or ripeness, for change. In outlining the details of this step of the process, we offer a few guiding questions (see below) that an initial, exploratory leadership team may wish to ask and answer as part of the process of (a) deciding if a disciplinary literacy professional learning initiative is appropriate at a particular point in time, and (b) designing a context-specific disciplinary literacy professional learning initiative. Asking and answering these essential questions is a first step in determining whether the time is right for an initiative, and what actions to take in order to ripen the situation to make an initiative more feasible.

Questions to ask before launching a disciplinary literacy professional learning initiative

- What do we already know about literacy teaching and learning in our school?
  - What professional development have we already engaged in around literacy or disciplinary literacy? What did we learn and what were the results?
  - Have we conducted a literacy-focused needs assessment recently?
  - Do we know our own strengths and weaknesses related to literacy teaching and learning?
  - How common are our strengths and weaknesses across departments, content areas, and grade levels?
  - Would teachers, leaders, students, and families all agree on our strengths and weaknesses?
  - Are there particular pockets of teachers or teams that seem most ready to engage in disciplinary literacy professional learning?
- What do we already know about excellent professional learning?

- Which professional learning structures (e.g., PLCs, collaborative planning/learning time, teacher leaders, instructional coaching, teacher access to professional materials, contracted experts) are already in place in our school?
- Which new professional learning structures and resources might we need to put into place *before* we begin a large-scale initiative?
- Which new structures might be most effective, given our school context?
- What experience do our teachers and teams have with engaging in inquiry-focused professional learning?
- What experiences with leadership or teacher leadership do our teachers have?
- What facilitation skills do our teachers already possess?
- Which skills may need to be bolstered before launching a larger initiative?

- Is the timing right? Is disciplinary literacy a ripe issue in our school?
  - Is there widespread agreement that students need more support with disciplinary literacy skills or literacy skills more broadly?
  - Is there a shared understanding of what "disciplinary literacy" means?
  - Is there broad-based willingness to engage in change processes around disciplinary literacy?
  - What work might we need to do in order to ripen the context and create a shared understanding of our school's strengths and needs?

- What funding and resources might be necessary?
  - Do we already possess the resources to launch an initiative?
  - Do we need to seek external funding, and if so, what are the pros and cons of doing so?
  - How might different levels of funding shape the structure and timing of a particular initiative?
  - When funding is scarce, is there agreement about spending funds on this type of initiative?

- How well does our community understand the processes of adaptive change?
  - Do we understand that this model relies on experimentation, reflection, and revision, and that change is not a linear process?

- How might teachers and others respond to a change process that relies on them to collaboratively develop new ideas and practices as opposed to looking to experts for information?
- Do we need to produce particular student achievement gains in order to support a particular professional learning initiative?
- What internal and external pressures might dictate how fast or slow we're able to work?

- To what extent and how might we evaluate a professional learning project?
  - To whom are we most accountable?
  - What kinds of data and evidence must we prepare to collect? (Note: this almost always needs to be decided before the project begins.)
  - How do we want to tell the story of our work?

- In what ways does this initiative interact with and come into balance with other work in our school community?
  - How do we see this initiative balancing with other improvement efforts that are currently underway?
  - Will this initiative provide professional balance for those involved, or is there the danger of initiative overload or burnout?
  - Does the idea of this initiative energize teachers and play to their strengths or growing edges?
  - Are the priorities of the community in line with this initiative?
  - What are our blind spots? What else are we not considering?

The questions above are designed to be suggestive, rather than prescriptive. Each school will necessarily ask and answer a slightly different set of questions, ones that are context specific and that reflect the particular strengths and challenges of each school community. The answers to these questions will help determine whether an action space might be opened to do this work. However, you may notice that the overarching categories of questions reflect key factors influencing the eventual timing, duration, and intensity of any given initiative. We dive into more fine-grained versions of these questions in chapter 5, as we outline how to engage in a context-specific needs assessment and project design process. But first, we note that *who* is asking and answering these questions will shape the answers. Thus, we turn to the *who* in the next section.

Collaborative from the very beginning

An initial leadership team may be asking and answering the questions above. This is by design. We have found that, across disciplinary literacy professional learning projects, the most successful initiatives begin with the formation of a leadership team to explore, discuss, and design a disciplinary literacy professional learning initiative. In a smaller school, this team may be quite small, for example, a middle school principal meeting with two trusted teacher leaders (representing different content areas) and a reading specialist. In a larger, comprehensive high school we worked with, the initial disciplinary literacy leadership team included ten people: department heads, teacher leaders, administrators, specialists, and outside consultants. While the size of the team may vary (we know of one high school that formed a team of over twenty people), we encourage you to aim for a team of about six to ten people. Include enough members to represent various stakeholders' interests in the community, but not so many as to bring decision making to a halt. The composition of the initial team is key. It is critical to include at least one administrator or school leader with decision-making power, representatives from various content-area departments (e.g., English language arts, math, social studies), at least one specialist (e.g., a reading specialist or special educator), and perhaps an outside consultant or district representative. Ideally, the team would have the ability to make genuine, actionable recommendations to school and district leaders, so team representatives should be aware of and careful with the power of their proposals.

The purpose of beginning with a team-focused design process is threefold. By including multiple school community members in the original investigation and design process:

- You naturally begin the process of creating a larger schoolwide shared understanding of both the need for and result of a disciplinary literacy–focused initiative.
- You ensure that various perspectives are included in the design work, so that the needs of different groups of students, teachers, leaders, and specialists will be represented not only in the design phase, but also in the resulting project design.
- You signal to the entire community that this professional learning project is not just about literacy instruction, but about building the school's capacity to engage in team-focused self-study and productive problem solving.

While there is much talk of creating buy-in in the educational leadership literature, we far prefer the notion of *authentic engagement*. If a disciplinary literacy–focused professional learning initiative is meant to engage a large number of faculty, then beginning with an exploratory design team signals that community engagement is a fundamental goal. Moreover, if you are a school leader or department head who is convinced that a disciplinary literacy initiative is the key to your school's success, forming a design team will help you begin the work of sharing leadership, testing your own assumptions, and creating a slightly larger network of formal and informal leaders advocating for authentic adult learning experiences. Your broad coalition begins with the leadership team.

Once formed, the leadership team's first order of business is to answer a critical question: *is this the right time to embark on a disciplinary literacy–focused professional learning initiative?* All too often, as the common theory of school change suggests, educators fall in love with a new idea and launch themselves and their schools into a full-fledged professional learning and instructional change initiative without a clear theory of action for how the initiative will shift teacher thinking, teacher practice, and student learning. In chapter 2, we talked about understanding what is feasible in a particular school context, and the team can help with this discussion. The strength of a disciplinary literacy leadership and design team is that you will hear diverse perspectives on what "disciplinary literacy" currently means to community members, whether and when faculty will welcome a disciplinary literacy–focused professional learning initiative, and for which community members the issue is most ripe. Because of its importance at the outset of a disciplinary literacy initiative, let's tackle the issue of ripeness in more depth.

WAITING AND PLANNING FOR AN ACTION SPACE TO OPEN

Challenges that require adaptive change are usually large in scope, and after framing these challenges, it is clear that an easy solution does not exist. Instead, adaptive change builds on an organization's strengths through careful, thoughtful experimentation and new learning, often taking those involved outside their comfort zones. Teams usually launch the work of adaptive change with a clear sense of their goals, mission, values, and strengths or weaknesses, but without a singular or linear clear path for how to reach their goals. At other times, teams realize that their goals for change cannot be met with technical solutions alone and so begin the work of adaptive change. No matter how schools arrive at their adaptive change work, once launched, this type of learning is often without a clear end point, as there is no singular solution or practice that all teachers are working to achieve or implement on a set timeline.

For example, teachers and leaders in a school seeking to better support English language learners (ELLs) across content areas may enter into a multiyear adaptive change process in which they collaboratively explore ELLs' strengths and weaknesses, community connections, and responses to new instructional experiments. This process, while it will result in some new, widespread practices that are seen as effective, may not have a clearly demarcated end point. There is no one problem that the team will have solved at a particular point in time. Instead, there are layers of nuance that those involved are tackling, and teachers will inevitably find that some approaches work better with individual students at particular grade levels or with particular content. In other words, this work of school change is a process that is complex and ongoing. After all, you wouldn't want a school to necessarily say: "Well, November 5. That's the day we figured out how to solve this issue. Now we'll just do that forever, and I'm sure all our challenges are solved." Instead, you would want the school to establish continual systems of support in which teachers perpetually designed and refined instructional practices to support ELLs.

This is the case with disciplinary literacy. Teaching disciplinary literacy, and learning to teach with a disciplinary literacy stance, is an adaptive leadership and learning process. Leaders and teachers entering into a disciplinary literacy–focused professional learning initiative must embrace the fact that the best answers or solutions are likely those that school community members in consultation with outside experts and resources will invent, test, and refine. Furthermore, the invention, testing, and refinement process, once begun, may only be truly successful if sustained for a long time. Those involved must be ready for bumps in the road in the form of failures, retooling, and refocusing at various points along the way. The action space necessary to create this sort of change requires careful planning, especially if an initiative is going to last over time and sustain inventive work.

Given this, the question "Is this the right time for a disciplinary literacy–focused project?" becomes a serious one, with answers that imply either an effective investment of time and resources over time, or a short-term injection of resources that ultimately will be wasted. Heifetz et al. suggest that asking if an issue is "ripe" is one of the most important first steps in any adaptive change process, and ripeness is one way to determine not only whether a change process is feasible, but whether it is well positioned to make meaningful change.[5] They explain that issues that are generalized across a system are ripe, and discerning this ripeness is what indicates the next strategy steps to take. Issues that are not quite ripe can be ripened by enlisting stakeholders to get involved. Form a disciplinary literacy–focused leadership team and have its first order of business be to determine if the issue of disciplinary literacy is ripe, or in which pockets of the school it might be ripe. But how does a team do that?

Returning to McDonald's theory of "action space" provides us with a relatively straightforward framework that leadership teams can use to begin assessing whether and to what extent an issue is ripe enough to warrant a large-scale professional learning initiative.[6] The time is ripe for a disciplinary literacy–focused professional learning initiative to begin when an action space opens, allowing that work to take hold and spread. As action space theory suggests, when money, civic capacity, and professional capacity align around an idea for school change, an action space may open for that work.

Sometimes these three resources converge spontaneously or with the emergence of new policies or standards. For example, consider how Title I funding and policy changes spurred thousands of schools to reform elementary literacy teaching and learning, and to bring a more specific literacy focus to reading and writing in elementary classrooms. At other times, there is work that schools or teams need to undertake in order to ripen a situation and bolster one or more of McDonald's three resources and make a project feasible. For disciplinary literacy–focused leadership and design teams, we encourage early conversations focusing on Heifetz et al.'s and McDonald's two related ideas to answer these questions: "Is disciplinary literacy a *ripe* issue in our school? If so, for whom? And which key resources—money, civic capacity, and professional capacity—are already in place, and which will need to be bolstered to ripen the situation?" The box "Possible Discussion-Based Protocols to Guide Early Leadership Team Conversations" suggests tools to use in these conversations.

POSSIBLE DISCUSSION-BASED PROTOCOLS TO GUIDE EARLY LEADERSHIP TEAM CONVERSATIONS*

The Future Protocol

- This protocol helps a team imagine an ideal future, roughly five years in the future, and then plan backward to consider what steps might need to be taken now in order to reach that more perfect future. Teams might use this protocol to spur creative design thinking and surface potential roadblocks that might influence project design.

The Consultancy Protocol

- This protocol helps a team frame an educational dilemma (such as students' struggles with reading, writing, and communication skills in content-area classes) and provides a structure to begin expanding thinking and considering multiple professional learning options. This is an excellent protocol to build a group's capacity to engage in protocol-based work.

Data Driven Dialogue

- This is one of many protocols that help teams look at large swaths of data (conceptualized broadly as many types of student work, and quantitative and qualitative data). This protocol can be very useful (and easily adapted) when teams are looking at student work and achievement and making determinations about how to focus a particular professional learning project.

*All protocols are available on the School Reform Initiative website, http://www.schoolreforminitiative.org.

To illustrate this early planning process, consider the Snapshot of Practice "Early Disciplinary Literacy Professional Learning Design Conversations," from Brookline High School, as a group of teachers and leaders began early conversations about what would become their successful four-year disciplinary literacy–focused professional learning initiative.

SNAPSHOT OF PRACTICE
Early Disciplinary Literacy Professional Learning Design Conversations

For Jenee Ramos, an English teacher at Brookline High School (BHS), the initial idea for a disciplinary literacy project came from her work on the Literacy Project, a summer intervention program targeting freshmen students of color and students from low-income homes who also struggled with literacy tasks in their English classes. The teachers had developed a curriculum to support students with basic reading and writing, but they soon realized that both struggling and proficient readers at the school would benefit from literacy skills instruction in each of their subject classes. The only problem was that the staff lacked prior training on this kind of teaching and learning; moreover, the school had strong content-area silos and limited experience with professional learning teams, which might be an important design feature of a professional learning initiative.

For Gary Shiffman, BHS's social studies curriculum coordinator and department chair, the first idea for the initiative came from a two-day brainstorming session sponsored by a local school foundation, the 21st Century Fund. At that session, Gary discovered that content literacy was a "thing," and that improving students' skills in that thing might make them better and happier students overall. He took his discovery to Jenee, who already knew what he had learned. Together, they began to brainstorm ways to get other people at BHS talking and thinking about content literacy.

Jenee then reached out to Jacy Ippolito, a local university professor who was known for working on adolescent literacy professional learning initiatives. After two phone conversations, the group quickly agreed that a traditional professional development model (a string of professional development workshops, led by outside consultants, and delivered to a faculty of over 150 teachers at once) would simply be ineffective. Moreover, asking outside consultants to simply "coach" individual teachers or larger groups also made little practical sense. Instead, the group agreed that it might be more productive to form a small, exploratory leadership team to discuss over time the best way forward within a larger, more reform-oriented professional learning project.

Our first leadership meeting revealed a great deal. An initial cross-content area team of teachers, department heads, specialists, and administrators had gathered to begin discussing possibilities, and various departments were represented: English, social studies, science, special education, and so on. Quickly, the conversation turned to existing strengths and challenges. The school had been doing very well on state standardized tests, compared to neighboring schools and districts, and there was certainly no need to panic. However, several of the teachers and leaders in the room had been working for multiple years on the Literacy Project, and there seemed to be growing concern that the implementation of Common Core State Standards, coupled with a growing ELL and special education population, would result in more students than ever slipping through the cracks. The ten folks in the room clearly shared a passionate view that improved reading, writing, and communication skills in the content areas were a key to students' future success. But after a bit of probing, it became clear that this was not necessarily a widely shared priority across the school. The notion of "disciplinary literacy" was still very new, even to those eager participants on the leadership team. Thus, Jacy asked critical questions of the group: "Is now the right time to begin a larger disciplinary literacy professional learning initiative? Is the issue ripe enough for BHS?"

To answer that question, without naming it "action space," Jacy spent several sessions with the leadership team teasing out the three key levers of the action space theory. The team first considered the availability of financial resources. A combination of school funds, release time for teacher leaders, and small stipends provided by local nonprofit funders "might" be available to support a multiyear initiative. However, the team would have to apply specifically for grant money, with a clearly articulated professional learning model in hand. The availability of funds seemed contingent on figuring out the other components, so we moved on.

Next, we considered civic capacity—"Was disciplinary literacy a stance toward teaching and learning that the leaders, teachers, the school board, and families in the community would be interested in supporting?" Through conversation, it became clear that the popularity of the previous Literacy Project tutoring program, summer school programming, and other piecemeal support structures represented fairly widespread support for literacy-focused improvement efforts. The design team felt reasonably confident that the community would support, ideologically and financially, a multiyear disciplinary literacy effort aimed at bolstering both teachers' and students' specialized literacy skills in the content areas.

Finally, we considered teachers' professional capacity. Were teachers currently overwhelmed by existing initiatives? Or was there a groundswell of eager teachers ready to launch into a rigorous professional learning experience? And did that group have a baseline of skills and knowledge that would allow it to take up and experiment with new disciplinary literacy practices quickly? The answers varied, department by department, with some content-area groups seeming more ready than others to jump into a new project. While some members of the leadership team strongly advocated for all BHS teachers to participate in the project from the outset, it quickly became clear that such a move would result in many teachers feeling overwhelmed or that their energies were divided among too many priorities. For example, the math department at the time had just undertaken a massive curriculum writing project in order to realign its teaching to Common Core State Standards. It seemed clear that, while there was some interest in disciplinary literacy from that department's teachers, they would need to wait to get involved. Meanwhile, the social studies department head and teachers were already starting to explore some "reading like a historian" practices and strongly signaled their intent to jump into a bigger disciplinary literacy professional learning project. While professional capacity and interest varied, there appeared to be enough of a groundswell to support an initial project.

The leadership team's discussions, and answers to the aforementioned questions, signaled two things clearly: (1) the issue of disciplinary literacy was ripe in certain departments and for certain teachers, though not universally across the school; and (2) there was a good chance that an action space around disciplinary literacy could open, if a clearly articulated model was presented in a timely fashion to the school, district office, and local funders. Finally, during a "Future Protocol" with the leadership team (available on the School Reform Initiative website, www .schoolreforminitiative.org), the group members imagined themselves five years in the future and described what they had already accomplished with the Content-Area Reading Initiative before even recruiting a single teacher. Once the group was able to imagine the project and its results so clearly, the whole team got to work writing grants, recruiting teacher teams, and launching the project.

These early conversations and determinations of uneven ripeness greatly contributed to the final project design of two two-year cycles of learning (for a complete four-year project), which would allow for three content-area teams to participate in each cycle. Teams would be invited to apply to participate, which also allowed the leadership team to determine team readiness on a case-by-case basis. Finally, the theory of action came into focus—small teams of teachers inquiring into disciplinary literacy practices over time, testing and piloting new work, and then sharing the results of their efforts with their departmental colleagues. There were still many details to decide on, but the seeds for the larger professional learning project had been planted.

~Jenee Ramos, English teacher and English team leader, and Gary Shiffman,
Social Studies Curriculum Coordinator and Department Chair (design and
leadership team members), Content-Area Reading Initiative, Brookline
High School; Jacy Ippolito, educational consultant

Notice the following elements in the BHS story:

- a leadership and design team comprising multiple stakeholders representing various content areas, different levels of formal and informal leadership, and outside consultants to provide both perspective and guidance
- an early focus on trying to include *all* faculty in the project immediately, with a later shift in focus to looking for pockets of ripeness within departments where disciplinary literacy ideas were already percolating
- asking again and again whether and how money, civic capacity, and professional capacity might converge to create an action space that would offer a rich starting point for a larger, systemic shift toward disciplinary literacy teaching and learning

Only after determining general ripeness and whether a genuine action space might open did the BHS disciplinary literacy leadership and design team consider and plan further design elements. These design decisions are the focus of the next chapter.

In chapter 5, we move on to the next step of the disciplinary literacy professional learning sequence, the selection and design of strategic professional learning structures and systems. We will review in greater detail the ways in which PLCs, teacher leadership, inquiry, and other professional learning mechanisms are initially constructed.

CHAPTER 5

Assessing Needs and Identifying Levers for Change

WE TURN NOW to the next steps that a disciplinary literacy leadership team might take, step two in the framework–assessing needs and identifying levers for change. The assumption at this point in the process is that a leadership team has (1) already formed, and (2) determined that there is a good chance of an action space opening in which disciplinary literacy work might flourish. That is, the team has determined that money, civic capacity, and professional capacity will likely come together to support a robust professional learning initiative.

This is an exciting and also precarious point in the process of designing a disciplinary literacy initiative. The inclination might be to start putting dates on a calendar, selecting teams to participate in professional learning experiences, and hiring outside consultants to begin holding workshops. However, there are several worthwhile steps to take *before* jumping into planning workshops or assigning roles and responsibilities. If a team is not careful at this step of the process, it might end up designing an initiative that neither builds on existing organizational strengths nor addresses particular areas of student weakness. This is when the leadership team must engage in a careful needs assessment, or self-study process, in order to guide project design work.

In the sections that follow, we outline how teams can: (1) conduct a targeted assessment of student needs, (2) determine organizational strengths and weaknesses related to professional learning supports, and (3) begin to design an initiative that addresses needs and builds on organizational strengths. Each action not only increases the disciplinary literacy leadership team members' capacity to learn with and from each other, but also often results in a much stronger project design than might otherwise emerge. We begin with the targeted needs assessment.

CONDUCTING AN EFFICIENT NEEDS ASSESSMENT

Conducting a targeted assessment of student learning and needs is one way in which a school and disciplinary literacy leadership team can ensure that the issue of disciplinary literacy is ready for attention. This can produce clear evidence justifying the reason for a robust professional learning initiative. While many schools engage in regular self-study processes, such as reviewing student achievement data, we advocate strongly for a targeted needs assessment process as one of the first orders of business for the newly formed disciplinary literacy leadership team. By targeted, we mean that the process should keep a laserlike focus on instructional practices and student learning related specifically to reading, writing, and communication in the content areas. While teacher satisfaction levels, student motivation, attendance rates, and so on might all be of great interest to various stakeholders in a school community, a disciplinary literacy leadership team needs to ensure that it does not lose sight of the reason for the self-study at hand–to determine which particular student and teacher needs the team will design the resulting initiative to address. If the needs assessment process is too broad or takes too long to conduct, it loses a great deal of its power to justify and shape a particular disciplinary literacy professional learning initiative. It loses the potential to create and support a particular action space.

   While leadership teams engage in a variety of self-study strategies, we have often seen teams rely on a combination of the following methodologies to give insight into student learning and achievement:

- collecting and analyzing representative student work
- interviewing teachers, students, and/or school leaders
- conducting focus groups with teachers, students, families, and/or school leaders
- surveying teachers, students, and/or school leaders

- analyzing existing documents (e.g., looking at teacher-created unit and lesson plans)
- reviewing available student literacy achievement data

The needs assessment methodologies the team chooses will depend on each team's comfort and familiarity with these collection and analysis techniques, the size and configuration of school personnel, the amount of time the team wants to devote to the process, and the size and capacity of the leadership team itself.

One of the larger disciplinary literacy leadership teams we have encountered included seventeen teachers and leaders across grades eight through twelve, including representatives from all content areas (including world languages and specialists). The team was able, given its size and the skill sets of its members, to conduct a multi-month, comprehensive, schoolwide needs assessment that included all of the aforementioned methodologies.[1] However, a self-study of this size and scope is rare. Most teams opt for a more streamlined, targeted process that focuses on one or two methodologies, several content areas, and a few specific literacy domains (e.g., reading comprehension, academic vocabulary, and writing). Most self-studies last anywhere from a few weeks to two months.

Recently, Rita Bean and Jacy Ippolito proposed a streamlined needs assessment process that we have adapted and outlined in the box "The Needs Assessment Process."[2] Of course, each disciplinary literacy leadership team must design and agree on its own steps; however, the six steps listed in the box provide a general scope and sequence as a starting point.

THE NEEDS ASSESSMENT PROCESS

1. *Identify the goals of the needs assessment.* First, the leadership team determines whether it needs a disciplinary literacy professional learning initiative and which specific areas it might address.
2. *Select or design preliminary needs assessment tool(s) to meet team goals.* The team decides on the scope of the needs assessment process and reviews possible data collection tools (such as the Content-Area Literacy Survey, described in the appendix at the end of this chapter), or begins to design a school-specific survey, or set of interview and focus group protocols.
3. *Determine existing sources of data.* The team identifies a variety of available student achievement data (e.g., state standardized tests,

school-specific formative assessment data, individual students' diagnostic assessment data, and so on) as well as swaths of student work, teacher lesson plans, or other teacher- or student-generated work products.

4. *Determine how to collect new data.* The team finalizes which specific methodologies (surveys, interviews, focus groups, document analyses, and so on) they will employ to collect new data to answer specific self-study questions.

5. *Decide on audiences to consult.* The team needs to identify which groups it wants to target in its needs assessment work: students, teachers, specialists, leaders, families, and so on. It will likely not target all audiences at once. The team will need to apprise each targeted audience of any final needs assessment results or reports.

6. *Analyze and report on data.* Finally, the team must sift through evidence it has collected, articulate a set of clear findings, decide on a format and process for reporting the findings, and communicate the results of the assessment project in a succinct and timely manner.[3]

Of the six needs assessment steps outlined in the box, identifying the goals (step one) is perhaps the most important. Most needs assessment work begins with several overarching questions designed to help teams learn more about how students and teachers are working within particular literacy-focused domains. For example, a team might ask the following:

- How do students describe the reading and writing tasks they complete in various content-area classes?
- Do students think that they are receiving enough support for writing in content-area classes?
- How do classrooms address academic vocabulary? Within particular content-area classes? Equally across classes?
- To what extent do faculty feel prepared to teach reading, writing, and communication within their content-area classes?

By beginning with a handful of targeted questions, teams position themselves to gather existing data as well as select one or two methodologies to help collect and analyze new, related information. For example, to answer the questions above, we might suggest designing and delivering matching teacher and student surveys, asking similar questions of both groups so that the team might compare results. Reviewing existing student achievement data and/or looking at a broad swath of student writing might help to corroborate or refute survey findings. By narrowing the focus of the needs assessment, teams will be able to dig deeper into specific areas of interest, as opposed to a scattershot approach that may not result in much new learning. Importantly, and as is the case with most social science research, self-study methods for collecting and analyzing relevant data should connect closely to the number and types of questions asked.

Another consideration is *how* the disciplinary literacy leadership team will analyze data that have been gathered or collected. Just as important as *what* information is collected, *how* the team goes about analyzing and reporting findings signals a great deal to the entire school community. We strongly urge teams to utilize structured conversations or discussion-based protocols to support data analysis and reporting phases of the work.[4] Protocols help leadership teams prevent snap judgments, surface their own assumptions about teaching and learning, and ultimately make strong evidence-based recommendations about the next steps for professional learning.

Regardless of the specific details of each leadership team's needs assessment process, the end results are often similar: a few identified areas in which teachers and students are quite strong, and a few identified areas in which teachers and students could use a fair bit of additional support. The seeds of a disciplinary literacy professional learning initiative can be found in these needs assessment results. While there may be one or two surprising results of the process, teams often report that it confirms many of their early suspicions–"Yes, we thought that our students needed more support with academic vocabulary." The key, however, is that now the leadership team has a fair bit of evidence to support initial hunches. Also, the process not only allows the team to build its own investigative and decision-making skills, but also provides a wealth of evidence to share with stakeholders and decision makers in the community who will need to invest time, energy, and money in the new initiative. Thus, the needs assessment process is a critical step in building broad, well-reasoned support for a disciplinary literacy professional learning initiative.

However, simply identifying teaching and learning strengths and weaknesses is not enough. To design a successful initiative, a leadership team must also assess organizational and professional learning strengths and weaknesses as the final part of the self-study process. We highly recommend that leadership teams focus some attention on organizational strengths and weaknesses related to professional learning supports. We address this idea briefly in the following section.

BEYOND TEACHING AND LEARNING: REVIEWING ORGANIZATIONAL AND PROFESSIONAL LEARNING STRENGTHS AND WEAKNESSES

Many leadership teams jump right from reviewing teaching and learning strengths and weaknesses to designing a professional learning initiative, filled with various mechanisms such as PLCs, instructional coaching, or instructional rounds. Teams that make this move are missing one essential ingredient, however. They are forgetting that teaching and learning strengths and weaknesses do not always signal which organizational or professional learning strengths or weaknesses exist in the school. Every school has a culture and structure that differently supports professional learning and collaboration, and our framework relies on a thoughtful combination of three complex structures: PLCs, collaborative inquiry, and teacher leadership. If a disciplinary literacy leadership team is not careful to review existing structures and supports, and the degree to which each is fully functional, then designing a disciplinary literacy professional learning initiative around fictional or faulty collaboration structures becomes a real possibility.

The classic example is the school that touts its PLC time, when teams of grade-level teachers are supposedly meeting and refining instructional practices together, only to find out upon closer inspection that the teams are not really meeting. Or perhaps they are meeting, but not really talking about teaching and learning. In this example, administrators might quickly advise that the primary learning about disciplinary literacy happen within grade-level PLCs. This might be less than ideal, though, if teachers in the school have little experience with or support for engaging deeply in PLC work. They might not be using discussion-based protocols. They may not have clearly designated facilitators. They might not use well-articulated meeting agendas. Though PLC time exists in such a school, it might need a good deal of bolstering before it can fully support the weight of a new initiative. As we noted in chapter 2, PLCs can be a powerful professional learning mechanism. But in a school where teachers traditionally

view PLC time as a superficial or empty activity, pinning the success of a bud-
ding disciplinary literacy project on effective use of PLC time could be quite
detrimental.

Thus, we recommend that toward the end of the needs assessment process,
focused initially on teaching and learning, that the disciplinary literacy leadership team investigate which professional learning and collaboration structures
the school is already using meaningfully. Which structures does it need to
develop before or during the early phases of the disciplinary literacy project?
Several tools and checklists can guide this kind of organizational review (see
the appendix "Resources to Consult When Conducting a Literacy Needs Assessment" at the end of this chapter). We also provide a quick checklist to guide
initial reviews in table 5.1.

We have seen our combination of three structures—PLCs, teacher leaders,
and collaborative inquiry—work well for supporting this type of work, but a team
could also smartly leverage other professional learning structures for support.
The team can uncover all this in a thoughtful organizational and professional
learning assessment process.

LEVEL-HEADED DESIGN WORK: BALANCING STRUCTURE, PROCESS, AND FACILITATION

After considering strengths and areas of growth for both literacy-focused teaching and learning, as well as professional learning and collaboration structures,
disciplinary literacy leadership teams begin the process of actually *designing* a
new initiative. Often, outside advice (from consultants or district-level administrators and coaches) supports their design work. This work is also often framed
in terms of a grant-writing endeavor to apply for supplemental funds in support
of a clearly articulated professional learning model. What is similar across all
work at this stage of development is the determination of specific professional
learning structures that build on existing organizational strengths and shore up
any potential weaknesses.

In our own research about the design and sustainability of disciplinary literacy professional learning initiatives, we have found a need for a level-headed
balance between *structure*, *process*, and *facilitation*.[5] We review each of these
areas briefly.

TABLE 5.1 Professional learning and collaboration structures to support disciplinary literacy work

	Not present	Present but not functioning as expected	Present and functioning	Functional with some room for improvement	Fully functional
PLCs					
Critical friends groups or other intentional learning communities					
Teacher leaders					
Inquiry-based group learning					
Instructional coaching					
Peer coaching					
Teacher mentoring					
Learning walks/ instructional rounds					
Professional development workshops					
Collaboration time					
Teacher teams					

Designing with structure in mind

One major design consideration is which structural mechanisms are going to bring faculty together to learn about and pilot new disciplinary literacy instructional practices. PLCs are excellent structural options that help teachers regularly meet, debrief, and refine their work together. However, PLCs may not be the right structure for a particular school. They may fare less well in smaller schools (or perhaps rural schools) with fewer faculty at each grade level or in each content area. PLCs may not be successful in schools with a checkered past using that particular structure. As in our previous example, if a school has been superficially using PLCs for some time, it may be difficult to switch gears and embed a new professional learning project in those less-than-stellar structures. This is when a disciplinary literacy leadership team will need to make some tough decisions about when and how to bring teachers together in meaningful ways.

Structural design decisions include:

- What initial time will faculty have to begin their professional learning experience?
  - A summer institute?
  - A series of workshops during the year?
  - Online modules and independent readings?

- What time will faculty have to do their learning together across the initiative?
  - Collaborative learning time during the school day?
  - Before or after school meetings?
  - Strategic use of grade-level or departmental meeting times?
  - Dedicated professional development time?

- Which and how many faculty need to meet regularly to learn together and pilot new work?
  - Content-area teams or cross-content area teams?
  - Grade-level teams or cross-grade-level teams?
  - How and when might specialists, special educators, instructional coaches, librarians, and/or administrators be included?

- How much time will be needed to maintain momentum?
  - Weekly meetings?
  - Every other week?
  - Monthly?

- How and when will personnel other than teachers be included in the work?
  - School-based coaches?
  - School leaders?
  - District-level leaders and/or coaches?
  - Outside and/or university-level consultants?

- Beyond inquiry cycles, what other structures will teams use to learn together?
  - Instructional or peer coaching?
  - Learning walks, classroom observations, or instructional rounds?
  - Lab classrooms?

- How and when will teams of teachers share their learning and work with others?
  - Throughout the project?
  - At the end of the project?
  - Within or across departments?

Designing with process in mind

Beyond structural considerations, procedural elements must be taken into account in the early design of any disciplinary literacy professional learning project. Once the leadership team and participants determine who and how often educators are meeting together, it is critical to consider *how* learning will happen within those structures. Our own research and experience suggests that an inquiry-focused approach may be best, with teams of teachers engaging in a series of inquiry cycles focused on various domains of disciplinary literacy (e.g., discipline-specific reading comprehension, academic language, discussion, writing, etc.). However, if teams have little to no training or experience in inquiry-based professional learning, then the disciplinary literacy leadership team may wish to design a slightly different mechanism or provide some early experiences that support inquiry-focused work.

Process design decisions include:

- How much experience do teachers have in self-guided inquiry work?
  - A great deal?
  - A little?
  - None?

- How much autonomy will teams have in engaging in self-determined inquiry cycles?
  - Will teams have complete freedom to explore?
  - Will teams coordinate inquiry cycles and explore similar topics together?
  - Will teams begin and end inquiry cycles at the same times, or will they have more freedom?

- How much will teams balance inquiry with delivery of new products?
  - Will teams have complete freedom to inquire into new practices, without organizational expectations about creating new products or routines?
  - Will teams be asked to deliver or present products of inquiry work at set times and places (e.g., at the end of each marking period within content-area departments)?
  - Will they videotape instruction and debrief together?
  - Will they use protocol-based design and problem-solving discussions?

- How will participants share their work with others who did not participate in the project?
  - Department or other meeting structures?
  - Teacher mentoring?
  - Materials distribution?

Designing with facilitation in mind

Now we turn our attention to facilitation. While we offer several excellent resources in the appendix related to facilitation, including books and tools focused on discussion-based protocols and collaborative decision making, we often find that clear design work attending to facilitation makes a big difference in the end results of any disciplinary literacy professional learning initiative. For example, we see incredible differences between projects that rely on teacher leaders to craft meeting agendas and guide group discussions using discussion-based protocols and projects that do not specify how to facilitate meetings, leaving each individual group to fend for itself. The inclusion of facilitators of disciplinary literacy-focused inquiry work has been shown to support a number of structural and procedural design elements.[6] However, teacher leaders who facilitate group learning may not be a possibility for all schools due to union contracts, a small faculty, or lack of training and support mechanisms. Therefore, we list a few potential design decisions related to facilitation for disciplinary literacy leadership teams to consider.

Facilitation design decisions include:

- Will designated teacher leaders guide each group and facilitate learning?
  - Do teacher leaders already exist in the school? Within content-area departments, or within grade levels?

- Do existing instructional coaches or specialists already have training and skills in facilitation, which can be drawn upon in the new project?
- Will new teacher leaders need additional training and support?

- Do faculty members already have experience with agendas and structured conversations?
  - To what extent will faculty in the initiative need training and support in the creation and use of agendas and discussion-based protocols?
  - Will facilitation responsibilities only reside with group leaders? Or will these responsibilities rotate?

These questions are suggestions, not prescriptions. They provide a starting point for teams to consider structural, procedural, and facilitation decisions that will naturally arise in the design of a new disciplinary literacy professional learning project. Ultimately, the decisions that the leadership team makes—in response to identified strengths and weaknesses related to teaching and learning, as well as professional learning and collaboration—will dictate the size, scope, cost, and sustainability of the resulting professional learning initiative. Moreover, the early decision that disciplinary literacy is an issue ready for exploration in the school may in fact be subverted by the needs assessment process. The leadership team may realize that there are simply not enough existing structural, procedural, or facilitation supports to initiate and sustain a full-fledged project. This has certainly been the case in some schools where we have worked. After an initial, exploratory, needs assessment process, the school has decided that it has some preliminary structural, procedural, or facilitation work to do before actually designing and beginning a larger disciplinary literacy professional learning initiative. In such cases, disciplinary literacy leadership teams often decide to slow their design process and instead advocate for the establishment of a few key foundational elements (e.g., workshops in facilitation and inquiry-based learning, training for teacher leaders, the establishment of a PLC or common planning time, and so on).

As an illustration of the flexibility required during the assessment and design phases of this process, consider the structural decisions made by the leadership team in Acton-Boxborough, Massachusetts, in the Snapshot of Practice "Different Structures for Different Initiatives." As you read the quick description of the project's design from the perspective of one of the consulting coaches—Jenny Jacobs, now an assistant professor at Wheelock College in Boston—notice how the design choices differ from the snapshot of the Content-Area Reading Initiative at Brookline High School in chapter 4.

SNAPSHOT OF PRACTICE
Different Structures for Different Initiatives

The multiyear disciplinary literacy initiative in Acton-Boxborough, Massachusetts, presented two new design challenges that required adaptation of the model my colleagues and I have typically used in consulting with districts. We approach our work as disciplinary literacy coaches with some core ideas about what has worked best in the past, but also with the flexibility to meet teams where they are.

The first was the timeline. In other districts (such as Brookline, Massachusetts), we had launched projects with a weeklong summer institute where we built a sense of community while studying the "what" of disciplinary literacy. This model had always given us a solid base on which to build so that our ideas and intentions did not get lost in the craziness of the school year. Due to a number of logistical factors, Acton-Boxborough asked us to roll out the disciplinary literacy content over the course of eight sessions during the school year, without a summer institute. As outside consultants, we wondered how this might affect our work. Would teachers have the energy during the school year to contemplate some of the bigger paradigm shifts a disciplinary literacy approach demands? Would they get enough time together to build that cohort feeling that we noticed at the end of our summer institutes? While we felt the lack of the summer institute at times, we alternately found many new opportunities to try out ideas right away. Introducing content across the year allowed us to implement new ideas quickly and play, for example, with the adapted vocabulary or discussion strategies we worked on together, as opposed to having to wait and hold onto summer learning until fall.

The second major design decision was not to designate teacher leaders. We had found in our previous work that assigning a teacher leader catalyzed the work, facilitating communication between the coaches, administration, and teachers. Our district partners on this project preferred to maintain a more horizontal relationship among teachers. Again, we were wary: Would lack of a clear liaison among teachers interfere with our ability to get teacher input on our planning? Would this slow down our communication with participants in general?

Over the course of the first year, we found that modifying our five-day summer institute to fit eight days during the school year was a huge challenge. The timeline had been designed with three full days and five half days, so that we technically had the same number of hours as we would have during a summer institute. We quickly realized, though, that the work to be done simply looked very different. Teachers in October and November were reading and discussing the same content as we do on the first two days of our summer institute, but with a very different focus. Teams needed much more time to digest and discuss practical applications of the work right away. The sense of urgency around how to do this right, and what it meant for one teacher's struggling reader or another teacher's critique of a school policy, was much more palpable. We found that we covered about half of the topics that we normally did in the summer, with much more depth and more opportunities for immediate implementation—and, of course, it was a lot messier than talking in more abstract terms over the summer. Teachers brought in examples that perplexed us all, and we spent more time grappling with the application of, for example, an activity for choosing which words to teach. Things that often seemed straightforward in June felt less so when introduced and implemented midyear. In many ways, this was an advantage; being forced to really try out our new ideas actually allowed us to deepen our understanding of each new disciplinary literacy topic introduced.

In terms of teacher leadership, we found two things. First, perhaps not surprisingly, natural leaders emerged from the group. However, leadership was not evenly distributed. In the case of one high school social studies team, all three turned out to be strong leaders who each took on a particular aspect of disciplinary literacy and ended up bringing back their learning and ideas to their department. It was less clear among other groups whether anyone on the team would willingly step into a leadership position. We also found during the course of the first year that teachers balked at the term "leadership" and were reticent to accept being called literacy leaders, despite the fact that these teams had applied for the opportunity to participate in a literacy leadership initiative. We speculated that this might be due to the fact that we had not laid out clear expectations for teacher leaders and modeled this process for the cohort. We worked during the second half of the first year, and well into year two, to demystify the term "leadership" and provide clear examples of what leadership might look like. It took a bit longer, but leaders did clearly emerge by the end of the second year.

~*Jenny Jacobs, EdD, Disciplinary Literacy Project Consultant, Acton-Boxborough Disciplinary Literacy Initiative, Acton-Boxborough Public Schools*

As we hope is clear from the Acton-Boxborough example, many disciplinary literacy initiative design decisions are made not only based on the findings of assessment work (e.g., teacher and student needs), but also based on what a district deems feasible. Compromises must be made based on finances, teachers' schedules, and for whom the issue is truly "ripe." In Acton-Boxborough, a summer institute was not possible for logistical reasons, nor was teacher leadership a notion already embedded in the district. Instead of waiting for those structures to naturally appear, however, the district moved forward with a modified project design (introducing new content across the first year of the initiative, and distributing and building leadership skills more slowly). Ultimately, these were the right design decisions for this project, for if the group had waited for other structures to emerge, it might have missed the window to begin the initiative at all. We learn again and again that designing an effective, context-specific disciplinary literacy initiative requires marrying initial ideas of how such projects work best to notions of what is feasible in a district. Such compromise requires flexibility and an authentic needs assessment process that uncovers important information.

We hope that this chapter has provided a few concrete suggestions for ways in which disciplinary literacy leadership teams might engage in meaningful self-study and early design work. In the next chapter, we continue our process by discussing how a leadership team might go about configuring effective teacher inquiry teams.

APPENDIX (Chapter 5)

Resources to Consult When Conducting a Literacy Needs Assessment

Books

- *Cultivating Coaching Mindsets: An Action Guide for Literacy Leaders*, by Rita M. Bean and Jacy Ippolito (West Palm Beach, FL: Learning Sciences International, 2016). Chapters 8 and 9 of this book focus on literacy-related assessment work in schools, including conducting targeted needs assessments. In chapter 12, the authors share a case of Hudson High School, and how their literacy leadership team conducted a disciplinary literacy self-study process.

- *Reading Specialists and Literacy Coaches in the Real World* (3rd ed.), by Mary Ellen Vogt and Brenda A. Shearer (Long Grove, IL: Waveland Press, 2016). While this book may be aimed specifically at reading specialists and literacy coaches, chapter 4 provides an excellent overview on designing and conducting a targeted literacy needs assessments, as well as developing a literacy-related professional learning plan.

- *The Power of Protocols: An Educator's Guide to Better Practice* (3rd ed.), by Joseph P. McDonald, Nancy Mohr, Alan Dichter, and Elizabeth C. McDonald (New York: Teachers College Press, 2013). This foundational book supports groups of educators wishing to use structured conversations, or *protocols*, to guide data analysis, problem-solving, design, and decision-making conversations.

- *Meeting Wise: Making the Most of Collaborative Time for Educators*, by Kathryn P. Boudett and Elizabeth A. City (Cambridge, MA: Harvard Education Press, 2014). A quick resource guide supporting team leaders and all those who are helping to set group norms, craft meeting agendas, and support groups of educators in data analysis and decision making.

- *The Facilitator's Guide to Participatory Decision-Making* (3rd ed.), by Sam Kaner and colleagues (San Francisco: Jossey Bass, 2014). The single best resource focused on how to help groups reach consensus-driven decisions.

Tools

- The Content-Area Literacy Survey (http://adlitpd.org/category/assess/). This online, free Google Form survey tool is a starting point for any middle or high school team wishing to create a disciplinary literacy-focused survey. With various components concentrating on teacher or student experiences and multiple literacy domains (e.g., vocabulary, comprehension, writing, etc.), this is a highly modifiable tool that teams can use to begin their needs assessment work.

- National Center for Literacy Education, Framework for Capacity Building, Asset Inventory (http://bit.ly/ncleassetinv). From the report *Remodeling Literacy Learning Together: Paths to Standards Implementation* (Urbana, IL: National Council of Teachers of English, 2014), p. 33, the asset inventory helps groups determine the extent to which teams in their schools are doing well with deprivatizing practice, enacting shared agreements, creating a collaborative culture, maintaining an inquiry stance, using evidence effectively, and supporting collaboration systematically.
- Professional Learning Communities Survey provided by the School Reform Initiative (http://school reforminitiative.org/doc/plc_survey.pdf). This brief tool supports groups in identifying areas of strength and weakness related to key elements of professional learning community and collaborative work.

Discussion-Based Protocols

- Data Driven Dialogue (http://schoolreforminitiative.org/doc/data_driven_ dialogue.pdf). This protocol helps participants first make sense of data without judgment and then draw conclusions.
- The Slice (http://schoolreforminitiative.org/doc/slice.pdf). This protocol guides participants to look at a slice of data from work samples across levels and classrooms.
- Interrogating the Slice (http://schoolreforminitiative.org/doc/interrogating_slice. pdf). This tool takes The Slice a step further by pushing participants to examine their own sensemaking closely as they examine data and draw conclusions.
- Gap Analysis (http://schoolreforminitiative.org/doc/gap_analysis.pdf). The purpose of this protocol is to identify gaps between beliefs and instructional practices and make connections between the two.
- More protocols, by category, found at the School Reform Initiative website (http://www.schoolreforminitiative.org/protocols/).

CHAPTER 6

Forming Teams of Content and/ or Cross-Content Area Teachers and Leaders

A DISCIPLINARY LITERACY leadership team that is able to discuss and collaboratively answer the questions in the planning phase is then ready to move on to the implementation phase of its initiative. The third step of our seven-step framework is to form teams of content and/or cross-content area teachers and leaders who will begin the professional learning work together. We turn our attention to team formation in this chapter.

This step is one of the most crucial in the project design and implementation process, because *who* enters into the project and *how* those participants are organized into teams can have a dramatic effect on the overall size, shape, pace, and success of the professional learning. In this chapter, we outline several related design decisions that leadership teams need to make. We also offer some potential options for the leadership team to consider as it determines and organizes project participants. But, first, it is important to consider several potential traps that leadership teams can fall into at this stage of the process.

We begin by outlining potential traps because we typically start our consulting conversations with schools and leadership teams here, as they often ask these questions first. Often, teachers and leaders have very well-reasoned, preexisting notions of how a disciplinary literacy professional learning initiative might proceed. Their questions require us to begin many of our consulting conversations with the caveats and potential traps to avoid during the design process, lest the projects start off on the wrong foot. So let's turn our attention to these traps first, to clear the way for new ideas about how to begin an initiative.

SEDUCTIVE TRAPS TO AVOID WHEN FORMING PROFESSIONAL LEARNING TEAMS

Leadership teams must recognize these traps and navigate them carefully so that the emerging project is not inadvertently constrained from the outset. These common traps often stem from good intentions that make them seductive and difficult to avoid, so project planners must either avoid them or be fully aware of potential pitfalls.

Potential trap #1: *Let's include everyone!*

One of the most common assertions we hear from school leaders and leadership teams at this stage of the design process is that they want to include *everyone* in the professional learning work. It is easy to understand this well-intentioned notion. Surely we want all faculty to benefit from professional learning about disciplinary literacy. Isn't it most powerful if all teachers in a school are aligned in their thinking and teaching of disciplinary literacy skills across grades and content areas? And what about accountability? Don't we want to increase participation by mandating that everyone engages in this work?

While including everyone in a disciplinary literacy project from the outset seems to make sense on several levels (alignment of practice, consistency across classrooms, etc.), the results of a "let's include everyone" decision can ultimately result in many faculty disengaging from both the content and the processes of professional learning work. Not all teachers in a school or department will be ready, willing, or able to engage effectively in collaborative inquiry around disciplinary literacy at the same time. Just as in classrooms where there is little differentiation according to students' learning needs, when we insist that all teachers engage in the exact same professional learning project and processes at the same time, we encounter a fair bit of disengagement or outright resistance.

Instead, we suggest that leadership teams think strategically about which teachers are primed to engage in the project now, knowing that other teachers can engage in this type of work later. Which departments, grade levels, and teachers are most ready to dig into this work? How can we design a project to let those who are ready begin and then intentionally spread the professional learning content and processes? How can we create small teams (six to eight teachers) who are truly going to collaborate regularly, as opposed to creating larger teams that might struggle to meet regularly, share their work, and be accountable to one another? These are the productive questions we hear leadership teams asking at this stage of the process.

Potential trap #2: *Everyone on a team must teach the same content, grade level, curriculum*

Another common trap is to think that the best (and only) teams are those comprising role-alike colleagues. We often hear from leadership teams (and some teacher teams) that the best professional learning can only take place when learning with or from colleagues who are teaching the same grade levels, subject matter, or curriculum. While we agree that a good deal of learning can happen in role-alike teams, we are skeptical that this configuration is the only or even best one. If one goal of a disciplinary literacy professional learning project is to push the boundaries of how we think about teaching students to read, write, and communicate within and across disciplines, cross-role or cross-grade teams of educators might be equally effective as role-alike teams. Teams including specialists, librarians, and teachers from across content areas and grade levels often have powerful conversations about similarities and differences in the disciplinary literacy skills needed in each of their domains. Furthermore, the particular perspectives of librarians and specialists (e.g., special educators, reading specialists, instructional coaches, technology specialists, and so on) truly inform the invention and refinement of classroom and schoolwide instructional practices (see the Snapshot of Practice "Including Librarians and Specialists on Teams," from two librarians involved in an initiative). Therefore, we caution leadership teams against being too restrictive when helping teams to form. Simultaneously, we do recognize that there are instances—particularly those when schools are under tremendous pressure to improve student outcomes—when forming role-alike teams might be more expeditious in terms of accomplishing results on a tight timeline.

> ## SNAPSHOT OF PRACTICE
> *Including Librarians and Specialists on Teams*

As librarians at Brookline High School, we initially considered applying to the Content-Area Reading Initiative as a separate "library team." However, realizing that our work is collaborative in nature, we reached out to other teams, hoping to have library representation on one or more teams. Recognizing that the librarians at Brookline High School work closely with the social studies department, mainly by developing lessons, teaching, and supporting student research, the social studies disciplinary literacy team embraced the idea of including a librarian, Ann Collins, on their proposed team. As a result of Ann's participation, the team developed a cycle on literacy skills related to the social studies research process. A second librarian, Shelley, voluntarily participated on the social studies team as well. Later in the year, Shelley formally joined the world languages team. Her work on that team focused on helping the team develop an independent reading component for Spanish classes (to be disseminated to other languages taught as well).

By the conclusion of the project, project participants were convinced more than ever that librarians, as interdisciplinary supporters of all types of literacy, should be integral members of disciplinary literacy teams. Our participation benefited the overall project in several specific ways:

- Since librarians work with teachers across disciplines and grade levels, they are natural "cross-pollinators." Much of the success of the disciplinary literacy project derived from bringing educators from different departments together to share strategies. During and after the project, we and our fellow librarians drew on our knowledge and experience of how each department handles challenges—from integrating independent reading, to teaching how to understand and mark up nonfiction texts, to using digital tools for teaching, creating, and presenting—and brought such concepts, strategies, and tools to other departments.

- Librarians are technology specialists, and as such, the Brookline High librarians were able to provide support to the outside consultants who led a discussion and offered readings focused on the role of technology in literacy work. This support was especially important as several members of disciplinary literacy project teams were skeptical of technology in this area, and were concerned about issues such as reading comprehension with digital versus print sources, and the literacy impact of time spent by adolescents on screens.

▪ Librarians are trained as curators and archivists of information. At Brookline High, we and our colleagues created a disciplinary literacy project website linked to the high school's main website as well as the library website. Each team has a page on the website where they and/or the librarian can archive the team's print and digital resources, such as background materials, readings, artifacts, lesson plans, and teaching tools. Ideally, such a website can support dialogue and the dissemination of information within and among teams, and will keep the disciplinary literacy project alive at Brookline High.

~Shelley Mains and Ann Collins, Librarians, Content-Area Reading Initiative, Brookline High School

Potential trap #3: *The principal (or other school-based leader) should choose participants*

While seductive, because it is efficient and carries a firm mandate from a formal leader, a strictly top-down process of selecting participants to engage in the professional learning project is one we caution against. In situations where teachers are "voluntold," or told they must volunteer to participate, the professional learning project begins with an impediment that must be overcome—teacher resentment and/or frustration at being told to participate in a project that may or may not make much sense to them. While not every project participant must be the most enthusiastic or eager volunteer, initial efforts to collaboratively co-construct the purpose and nature of the professional learning project with teachers helps generate authentic investment of teacher time and energy.

Teachers want to know that the upcoming project is going to result in deep learning for both adults and students, and that the school is going to sustain and support the project over time. Holding information sessions and facilitating collaborative design conversations with teams and teachers early on in the project design stage not only enrich the leadership team's design decisions, but also serve as a mechanism for creating interest and excitement about the upcoming project. Ultimately, the leadership team's selection of project participants is a balance between choosing teacher participants and seeking volunteers. If this balance is carefully struck, then the professional learning project begins with much more enthusiasm and energy than it might otherwise.

Potential trap #4: *Team leaders are assigned without consideration of team dynamics*

Last, we have found some school leaders or leadership teams eager to simply assign teacher leaders to guide the various teams engaged in the professional learning project. Again, this is a seductive option. It is expedient. Furthermore, many leaders and leadership teams have a good sense of which educators might make the best team leaders. However, the teacher leaders who guide the work of disciplinary literacy teams seem to be most successful when team members see them as both leaders and learners, as co-constructors of the experience.[1] Just like the formation of the teams themselves, the selection of team leaders can either support or hinder later team learning. We suggest that leadership teams carefully consider an alternative to simply assigning teacher leaders. A selection process in which teams have some voice in the assignment of team leaders, or even total autonomy in designating their own team leader/facilitator, can signal to teams that independence, autonomy, and teacher leadership are going to be prized in the professional learning initiative. Teams may feel freer to choose a team leader who is neither the most senior nor the most vocal in the group. Many of the teams with whom we have worked have wisely chosen second-stage teachers (those in their fourth to tenth year of teaching) as team leaders. These teachers have enough experience to ask great questions and guide team learning, but they are also early enough in their careers to naturally operate as co-learners in the group experience.

These design traps are just a few of the most common we have encountered at this stage in the process of designing and launching a disciplinary literacy professional learning initiative. We note these potential traps so that leadership teams might avoid being seduced by what is most expedient or what follows tradition and move through these questions into the process of assembling teams best situated for success. As the design process nears its end, and the project implementation phase is about to begin, we notice that leadership teams sometimes rush the final details of selecting participants, forming teams, and assigning team leaders.

FORMING TEAMS: THE BRIDGE BETWEEN DESIGN AND IMPLEMENTATION

We recommend taking the time necessary to form teams carefully, as well-formed teacher teams will lead to successful professional learning and increased student learning. Next we outline the three main decisions that leadership teams need to make at this stage in the design process.

Should teams be content-specific or cross-content?

One of the biggest determiners of how teams will ultimately engage in the professional learning work—in terms of collaborative processes and selection of inquiry topics—is the decision to form role-alike content-specific teams or cross-role cross-content teams. In some instances, schools might actually choose to focus mainly on role-alike or content-alike teams, with one or two members who fall outside the shared domain. For instance, as discussed above in the Snapshot of Practice, a social studies team might also include a school librarian in order to integrate a slightly different perspective on literacy in the discipline. But, it can be limiting to only consider forming role-alike content-area teams. Both types of teams (role-alike or cross-role) can thrive in a disciplinary literacy professional learning project; they simply end up engaging in the work in slightly different ways. Let's review some potential strengths and limitations of each design decision.

Creating content-specific teams can result in powerful professional learning. When role-alike groups of English, history, math, or science teachers meet regularly over a year or two to collaboratively investigate disciplinary literacy instructional practices, they can make great progress toward common habits of mind when reading, aligning curriculum, sharing assignments and assessments, and intertwining vocabulary and writing instruction. Meeting regularly with teachers across grade levels who share the same discipline-specific ways of reading, writing, and communicating can assist teams in aligning practices vertically across grade levels within a specific content area (e.g., ensuring that writing instruction and expectations in high school science classes across grade levels are aligned, which helps students build a common set of discipline-specific writing tools and methods). Content-specific teams are able to focus their attention fully on improving the ways that they model how historians, mathematicians, or scientists create knowledge, marshal evidence, or selectively attend to the most critical pieces of information in texts. Beyond shared content interests and expertise, content-specific teams also may easily agree on collaborative processes and methodologies (given their shared discipline-specific training). A group of science teachers might easily agree on piloting small instructional experiments in their classrooms, collecting data, and analyzing the results as a group. Alternately, a group of English teachers may quickly agree that collaboratively designing and piloting independent reading programs would be most effective. In content-specific teams, opportunities abound to engage in lesson study, to collaboratively design and pilot common units and lesson plans, to closely analyze discipline-specific reading and writing tasks, and to shift the way that larger content-area departments operate. Sometimes these procedural decisions can be more complicated in cross-content area teams.

For example, at Brookline High School, a content-specific team of math teachers was able to revamp the way that students engage in discipline-specific mathematical discussions, partly because their curriculum and instructional methods were similar enough that they could co-design open-ended questions, pilot various talk moves in their classes, observe one another's classes, and help each other to refine the work in a detailed manner that would have perhaps been more challenging in a cross-content area team. That team's work on math-specific discussion, vocabulary, writing, and reading instructional practices was then more readily adopted by the larger department. The group became a powerful constituency within the department, and had piloted enough of its work across classes and grade levels within the math department to demonstrate that its work was making a difference in students' mathematical reading, writing, and communication skills. This departmental influence might have been lessened if only one math teacher, as part of a cross-content team, attempted to bring new practices back to the math department to spur large-scale departmental change. Another example of the power of content-specific teams comes from Mary Angione, team leader of Brookline High's science disciplinary literacy team (see the Snapshot of Practice "The Power of High School Content-Specific Teams").

SNAPSHOT OF PRACTICE
The Power of High School Content-Specific Teams

When I set about creating a team, I intentionally sought out teachers from all three science subject areas: physics, biology, and chemistry. I also wanted a variety of levels represented: college preparatory, honors, advanced placement. I was able to assemble a team with a lot of collective teaching experience, so regardless of which level someone was teaching in a particular school year, that individual had likely taught another level at some point. Therefore, we understood the level-related challenges our fellow team members encountered in the classroom. We ended up appreciating the variety of ways that we might make adjustments in our practice along a continuum—from tiny changes that required little preparation and little class time, to more major overhauls of materials or our teaching method for certain topics. Smaller tweaks were generally the more common adjustments to practice in advanced classes, and the bigger changes were generally in college prep-level courses.

While there were certainly differences in emphasis or need for particular disciplinary literacy skills in the different science subject areas, there was a lot of commonality. Our conversations gave us an appreciation of the skill set and way of thinking that underlies success in any scientific discipline. Because our sequence of science courses is ninth-grade physics, tenth-grade chemistry, and eleventh-grade biology, the team naturally had teachers of different grade levels, since all required subject areas were represented. This allowed us, as a team, to begin to think about what a progression of skill might look like from ninth to eleventh grades. We were able to ask ourselves how we as a department might create some synergy if we were targeting particular skills in particular grades. The greatest strength of being on a content-specific team was learning and thinking together about how to translate theory into actual practice with our current students and our specific content.

Being a scientist, I think of every school and every classroom as something of a niche environment. There is no one-size-fits-all, ready-made strategy. I always found scholarly journal articles interesting and enlightening, but often felt frustrated and at a loss as to how to alter my practice. Working with other skilled, motivated science teachers, and being able to talk concretely at the detailed level of curriculum, helped me see new possibilities and make successful changes. I finally felt like I was getting the hang of embedding literacy instruction within my content teaching. For the team as a whole, it seemed like greater creativity and improvisation came as we gained experience and confidence. The team model allowed for a great cross-breeding of ideas and a forum for answering the question, "What does this really look like in my classroom at the level of a particular lesson plan?"

~Mary Angione, Chemistry teacher and Science Team Leader,
Content-Area Reading Initiative, Brookline High School

Alternately, cross-content area teams of teachers have several advantages over content-specific teams. First, cross-content area teams can often help each other to truly see the challenges posed by each of their discipline-specific texts. When role-alike teachers gather together, there is the possibility that (because they each have likely excelled within their discipline and focused their studies in that discipline both as early learners and as later professionals) they might struggle to tease apart the challenges posed by historical, mathematical, or scientific texts. Cross-content area teams are sometimes better equipped to help identify common or individual reading goals and challenges. When a math teacher analyzes a poem and when an English teacher solves a word problem about the volume of regular solids, each may be well positioned to illustrate how and why students might struggle through the discipline-specific texts. As a result of such conversations, members of cross-content area teams might be able to efficiently come to a consensus on which habits of mind and ways of reading, writing, and communicating are discipline specific and which are truly shared across domains. This kind of cross-content area team is well suited for aligning instruction across an entire grade-level (e.g., pairs of English, history, math, and science teachers form an eight-person team and investigate the ways in which they might share or differentiate reading, writing, and discussion instruction across an entire grade level).

Two other major benefits of forming cross-content area teams include focusing more on students' needs, and influencing instruction across a wide swath of the school. In our experience, we have found that cross-content area teams tend to focus a bit less on curriculum and a bit more on identifying and meeting students' needs across grade levels and content areas. Perhaps this is the result of the wider array of disciplinary training, instructional perspectives, and curricular goals in cross-content area teams. Often these diverse teams begin their inquiry by studying how students excel or struggle across content-area settings, searching for common patterns of behavior. As a result of these inquiry cycles, cross-content area teams tend to experiment with larger support systems for students (beyond just one or two content areas), for example, researching, designing, and piloting tiered instructional models to support students who struggle across content areas. Cross-content area teams also tend to want to influence entire grade levels or entire schools, as opposed to focusing on shifting the work within single departments. As cross-content area teams consider tiered instructional models, systems of support for students, and common instructional strategies across content areas, they often seek to influence grade-level or whole-school policies and practices. For more about cross-content area teams, see the Snapshot of Practice "The Power of Choosing Cross-Content Teams in Middle School," from a middle school disciplinary literacy initiative led by Joanna Lieberman, an English Language Arts K–8 Curriculum Coordinator, also in the public schools in Brookline, Massachusetts.

SNAPSHOT OF PRACTICE
The Power of Choosing Cross-Content Teams in Middle School

Our suburban-urban school district (Brookline Public Schools) has eight K–8 schools that feed into one two-thousand-student high school. Because of this configuration, the middle schools are quite small. Often, there are only one or two content-area teachers for each subject in a middle school. Collaboration happens more frequently across the middle school content areas than within each discipline itself. Increasingly in the last few years, curriculum coordinators and building administrators found themselves involved in difficult conversations with content-area teachers about middle school students' ability to read and write in these core classes. Over the last six years, the average proficiency rating on the state ELA test was 84 percent in sixth grade, 89 percent in seventh grade, and 91 percent in eighth grade. These numbers bested the state average, but still left many students behind, particularly students of color, low-income students, those with IEPs, and those with an ELL or former ELL designation. While there has been an effort to strengthen literacy instruction in K–5 classrooms and, to some extent, the sixth- to eighth-grade ELA classrooms, little attention has been paid to the literacy demands and the subsequent needs of students in the various disciplines (math, science, social studies, world languages, etc.).

In an effort to work within the small middle school structure, three curriculum coordinators wrote a grant to begin a disciplinary literacy initiative at the middle school level. The program called for the creation of teams of up to five cross-disciplinary teachers at four of the eight middle schools. Teachers volunteered to apply to each school-based team, completing a short application in which they expressed their motivation for working with colleagues on disciplinary literacy in their buildings. Those teachers who were interested in playing the role of team leader completed a separate application. Six of the eight middle schools expressed interest, and four of those submitted full-team applications to participate in the project. Principals and district leaders were informed of the plan, and some additional funding was secured to give stipends to teachers for work outside of school.

The project began in August with team leaders from each of the four schools attending a kickoff session with consultants Christina Dobbs and Jacy Ippolito. The session focused on an introduction to disciplinary literacy and some work on teacher leadership. The team leaders pledged to meet with their team members and provide an overview of the topic.

At the beginning of October, the entire group of twenty teachers met with consultants to begin studying the domains of disciplinary literacy. The first session offered an overview of disciplinary literacy and an introduction to the reading process as well as some time for the teams to work together to begin identifying a school-based area of need to explore throughout the year. Four weeks later, the second session explored academic vocabulary in greater depth and provided time for the teams to meet with the consultants. There are approximately six such days scheduled for the remainder of the year. Between professional development sessions, the teams meet for three hours a month outside of school time to research, talk, and refine their particular area of interest.

Teams have identified such diverse inquiry topics as multiple texts in social studies, ELA, and science; academic vocabulary in seventh- and eighth-grade classes; students' experiences of learning in science, math, social studies, and ELA; and exploring habits of mind and related reading strategies across disciplines in the eighth grade.

Although the work is in its early stages, the project has generated momentum in each of the buildings because of its multidisciplinary approach. In the past, teachers in different disciplines have collaborated on projects such as reading a historical fiction text in ELA that corresponds to a unit of study in social studies, but that work has focused largely on content-area connections. This project requires teachers to examine an area of adolescent literacy learning (e.g., academic vocabulary) that transcends all the disciplines and to consider how better understanding that particular domain in all those disciplines might have an impact on student achievement. We believe that students will benefit from having coherence in their instruction across disciplines. For example, if teachers in all content areas incorporate tier-two, or general, academic words into their instruction, students learn to recognize how these words function in each discipline, how they are alike and how they differ.

This type of inquiry has the potential to shift the perceived responsibility for students' literacy achievement from the ELA teacher alone to the entire middle school team. We anticipate that having all teachers work with students to improve their literacy learning across different classes will create a shared sense of responsibility for student achievement.

> ~Joanna Lieberman, English Language Arts K–8 Curriculum Coordinator,
> Middle School Disciplinary Literacy Initiative, Brookline Public Schools

The biggest limitations of each model—content-specific and cross-content area teams—include (respectively) potential myopia and potential floundering. In our experience, one of the biggest limitations of the content-specific teams is that they might focus too narrowly on their own content-area interests, limiting the consideration of rich connections *across* content-area classes. On the other hand, cross-content area teams might flounder at times, struggling to find a unifying inquiry topic that allows a wider range of content-area teachers, specialists, and librarians to find common ground. At times, cross-content area teams find themselves with less focus and struggling to produce instructional products that seem much easier for content-specific teams to construct.

Ultimately, logistical factors (e.g., funding opportunities; who can collaborate during the same blocks of time; which teams of teachers seem most ready to engage in professional learning together) may determine the formation of content-specific or cross-content area teams. Regardless, our recommendation is to ensure that whichever model a school chooses (including a combination of the two models), literacy leadership teams should be clear about the strengths and limitations of each design choice in order to provide the most effective supports moving forward. Project leaders will need to be ready to offer suggestions for how each type of team might capitalize on its strengths and slowly overcome potential limitations.

Are team members selected or invited to participate?

The second major decision at this stage of the design process is how team members will join the project. In small schools or departments, this decision may not be a big one, and truly everyone will be able to participate in the project. Alternately, in the larger, comprehensive high schools we have worked with, choosing who participates and designing a fair process for how participants enter the project can be one of the most challenging decisions. As we mentioned previously, the leadership team should avoid the potential design trap of automatically assuming that it is feasible or best for everyone to participate. If all teachers are to be part of the disciplinary literacy project, then a well-defined process should include teachers in the design of the project and explain to the entire school community the intent and nature of the work. In most settings, however, we recommend that smaller groups within the school community begin the project, with others included in the work over time as readiness and capacity grows across the school. Regardless of the scope of involvement, *how* teachers enter into the project can determine the enthusiasm and pace of the project from the outset.

On one end of the teacher-selection continuum is a top-down process wherein school leaders (the principal, assistant principal, department heads, literacy leadership team) ask particular teachers to join the project. The power of this design decision includes expediency, the formal authority of leadership, and the ability to carefully construct teams that leaders believe will collaborate effectively. In our experience, such top-down determination of involvement is most often effective in particular cases. If a school is underperforming and in danger of failing, top-down determination of participation in professional learning may be necessary in order to move into instructional improvement work as quickly as possible. If a school has already done the large-scale needs assessment and campaigning work to engage the entire school community in an analysis of student needs and the design of professional learning, then school leaders may have earned enough trust and support to simply create teams and determine participation. Last, when the school leaders approach individual teachers and ask them to participate because of specific skill sets they would bring to the project, we have seen great success.

This top-down approach has several big limitations, however. All too often school leaders and literacy leadership teams have not done quite enough groundwork to engage all faculty in the needs assessment and collaborative design process. Therefore, when school leaders assign teachers to the professional learning project, the teachers are caught unaware and feel that they've been "voluntold" to participate, without fully understanding the potential benefits of involvement in a project focused on disciplinary literacy. Alternately, school leaders are not always well positioned to know the interpersonal dynamics among faculty, and they sometimes craft teams with conflicting personalities that make collaboration challenging. Finally, when leaders assign teachers to teams without much input, the focus of the assignment can feel (to teachers) like a mandate for instructional improvement. In these cases, teachers might feel that they are being chosen because they are lacking skills, not because their expertise is valued.

On the other end of the decision continuum is a process designed to allow teachers to voluntarily participate in the upcoming professional learning initiative. The exact nature of the volunteering differs across projects, but the commonality that exists is genuine interest in participating in the project and full awareness of the responsibilities that participation brings. Whether teachers are asked to submit individual letters of interest, complete applications (see an example in the appendix at the end of this chapter, "Sample Team Member Application for Disciplinary Literacy Professional Learning Project"), send an e-mail to a school leader signaling interest, or whether teams are asked to apply together as groups, the purpose of this method is to truly engage the most interested faculty at the outset of the initiative. The theory of action here is that teams of the most enthusiastic faculty will be able to do good work in the earliest stages of the professional learning initiative and then will help spur interest and changes in practice with more wary colleagues over time. We have seen this sequence of events play out across more than a half-dozen school settings, from smaller middle schools to larger, comprehensive high schools. In each case, whether teachers were asked to formally apply as individuals or teams, or informally signal interest to a school leader, the resulting teams were able to begin their work efficiently and with great enthusiasm. Furthermore, in cases where more individuals and teams applied than the project could accommodate, leaders gave teachers and teams clear timelines of when another round of involvement would open and they might become a formal part of the project. While telling enthusiastic teachers to wait for the next round of professional learning can be tricky, if handled delicately, it can also create more interest in and enthusiasm for the initiative later.

Ultimately, across schools, we have found that a compromise between leaders simply assigning teachers and teachers participating on a completely volunteer basis makes sense in most schools. Some mechanism by which teachers can signal interest—coupled with a recommendation, vetting, and review process by the literacy leadership team or school leaders—can help ensure that the project is populated with individuals and teams that are going to carry the professional learning forward expediently and powerfully.

How many teams should be in the project?

A third decision is critical at this juncture—how many teams should engage in the professional learning initiative at the outset? This decision may be dictated largely by funding, space considerations, the number of existing initiatives that teams, grade levels, or departments are already engaged in, or other school-level contextual factors. While the other decisions in this chapter have had clearer pros, cons, and compromises, this decision is a bit less either/or, and much more scalable, depending on the exact purposes of the professional learning initiative and the resources available to support teams.

For instance, in schools that include *everyone* in the professional learning project, there are as many teams as there are departments and grade levels. In schools that make this decision, we have only seen great success when an adequate number of knowledgeable team leaders, trained in facilitation of small-group learning experiences, exist (e.g., team leaders trained in the use of discussion-based protocols, with knowledge of how to guide team inquiry processes). Alternately, in smaller, under-resourced schools, we have seen the decision made to start with just one or two teams of teachers to test the waters for a larger professional learning initiative in the future.

The most common number of teams that schools choose, across projects, seems to be in the range of three to six. Three to six teams engaging in the professional learning work together provide ample opportunities for both within and cross-team conversations and support. Project leaders can easily meet with team leaders, and team leaders are more able to learn with and from each other. If teams need to be released from teaching responsibilities in order to observe each other's classrooms or gather for an off-site day of professional learning, three to six teams (each comprising a handful of teachers) are far more manageable to convene than larger numbers. However, in settings where three to six teams join the professional learning project together, we have also seen rounds of professional learning implemented—with new teams of three to six teachers joining the project (either joining, or taking the place of the first teams) after a year or two. In this way, projects expand slowly and deliberately over time to ultimately spread the work across entire schools. However, to be effective with this model, the literacy leadership team needs to have a clear theory of action for how teams will rotate, join the project, and slowly spread the work over time.

PURPOSE IS KEY

In this chapter we have outlined some of the major decision points related to forming teams of content and/or cross-content area teachers. Before moving on to the next step in the framework for implementing disciplinary literacy professional learning initiatives, we want to give you one final thought. The *purpose* for the professional learning initiative needs first and foremost to guide each of the decisions outlined in this chapter. We have often seen logistical details, such as the alignment or misalignment of teacher collaboration time, guide large-scale decisions about who to involve in the professional learning project or how to form teams. We encourage disciplinary literacy leadership teams, as they are making key design decisions, to continually return to the guiding principles and purposes undergirding their original reasons for starting the project. What is driving the overall interest in starting such an intensive and long-lasting professional learning journey? Which design decisions are going to truly support the work over time? And which decisions can we live with, knowing that these types of professional learning initiatives often thrive over many years and that we don't have to achieve all goals with everyone instantly?

The *purpose* is key. When forming teams and beginning to consider the next stage of making meaning about disciplinary literacy practices (chapter 7), literacy leadership teams and project participants must continually voice *why* this project is so important and how each design decision furthers the overarching purposes of the larger initiative.

APPENDIX (Chapter 6)

Sample Team Member Application for Disciplinary Literacy Professional Learning Project*

Team Member / Team-Leader Application

Name: _____

Department: _____

If applying jointly, with whom? _____

1. Why do you want to be a member of a Departmental Literacy Team (or Team Leader)?

2. Why do you think you would be an effective member of a Departmental Literacy Team (or effective Team Leader)?

3. Your signature below indicates that you are prepared to commit to two years of participation in the project, and to fulfill all of the following responsibilities:

   - attend a weeklong summer institute on disciplinary literacy

   - participate in summer planning sessions with departmental teammates (3 days TBA)

   - attend and contribute to the success of weekly Departmental Literacy Team meetings

   - participate in four "days away" during the school year for professional learning

   - participate in mutual classroom observations (live and taped) and lesson demonstrations with other team members

   - read about disciplinary literacy; design curriculum and assessments; and learn from student work

_____   _____

Signature   Signature of Department Head

*Reprinted with permission from Jenee Ramos, Brookline High School.

CHAPTER 7

Making Initial Meaning of Disciplinary Literacy Principles and Practices

ONCE PARTICIPANTS are assembled for a disciplinary literacy initiative, it is time to get the work of collaboratively learning well and truly underway. Making smart decisions about starting the work can make an enormous difference in how people initially engage in the work of learning together about disciplinary literacy and how the momentum of this work will be shaped as implementation begins. In this chapter, we will discuss several items in step four of the framework: potential ways to begin the early learning that groups will conduct together, the literacy domains we have found to be helpful to teams as they begin their work, and the ways that groups might form and maintain their professional learning communities.

Carefully orchestrating the beginning of a project, with moves designed to support and engage participants, provides a strong foundation of collaboration over the long term.

THE POWER OF EARLY GROUP LEARNING ABOUT DISCIPLINARY LITERACY

As an initiative is getting off the ground, groups often find that doing some initial learning together forms an excellent launchpad for teams preparing to learn about disciplinary literacy. This learning can take a variety of shapes and structures, but the key is establishing a broad base of shared understanding in order to set the stage for inquiry cycles and collaborative learning. Because of the departmental nature of many secondary schools, and because teachers across disciplines are often trained differently, establishing a common set of understandings using a shared vocabulary that connects teachers from a variety of disciplines can be beneficial.

With regard to the content of this learning, there are two main areas to explore: literacy and collaboration. First, we'll discuss the literacy content we have found helpful to review in initial learning sessions. In our experience, doing some early exploration of disciplinary literacy domains can help establish a clear purpose for later collaborations. This injection of content learning early in a project gives teams a place to begin as they consider what they would like to improve in their own school contexts and classrooms. Furthermore, at this point in the professional learning process, it can be quite useful to invite external experts (e.g., district leaders, university consultants, etc.) to help guide early group learning experiences. Often an injection of outside expertise helps to jump-start group learning and set the stage for later inquiry.

But first, a caveat—we often work with content teachers whose experience engaging in literacy work focuses on using general strategies that have sometimes been advertised as the sole means for improving adolescents' reading, writing, and communication skills, as we discussed in chapter 1. Framing early group professional learning work as substantively different from such experiences is important. Disciplinary literacy, with its focus on improving skills that disciplines use to communicate, has a different agenda, one more closely related to the interests and improvement goals of teachers from a variety of content areas. Doing disciplinary literacy work in a math classroom is about improving math achievement, not simply using math as a means to improve reading (or reading to improve math, for that matter). If we expect genuine investment in disciplinary literacy professional learning initiatives, teachers must learn early that the projects are not about simply improving broad reading skills for language arts or other state assessments, but instead are about improving student skills in the disciplines.

Reframing teachers' conception of literacy instruction as disciplinary literacy instruction is foundational in helping to set up the team inquiries that will follow. Building on conceptions of the basic and intermediate literacy skills described by Timothy Shanahan and Cynthia Shanahan, disciplinary literacy is, in many ways, a newer pursuit than other topics teachers typically explore in professional learning.[1] In our view, disciplinary literacy requires teacher participants not only to learn about work that already exists on the topic, but also to adapt and invent their own new instructional strategies to support the specific needs that arise when their students and their disciplines meet.

Because it is a new idea in the field, the approach to professional learning around disciplinary literacy cannot consist solely of static workshops wherein someone simply presents known and tested instructional strategies to participants in workshops, with the expectation that teachers will then implement those strategies independently. Instead, when investigating disciplinary literacy instruction, teachers' learning needs to start with a foundation of emerging knowledge in the field. But this early review must also emphasize all that is yet to be discovered in the field, with a clear call for teachers to engage in the discovery and invention of new disciplinary literacy practices through collaboration.

This approach to professional learning—of laying a foundation upon which teachers themselves then build—represents a different paradigm for adult learning work in which teachers themselves are the creators of new knowledge and practice throughout the learning process. However, for this inquiry-driven, collaborative model to work, teachers need early, in-depth opportunities to learn about what is known about literacy in the disciplines. Thus, we endeavor to begin each professional learning project with the exploration of promising topics to guide teams' later exploration.

SETTING THE STAGE: TOPICS FOR EARLY EXPLORATION IN LITERACY AND COLLABORATION

Literacy first

Exploring this modern conception of disciplinary literacy and its relationship to more general skills is foundational, as it supports all later team inquiry work.

Teams often find the Shanahans' heuristic for understanding the increasing complexity and specificity of literacy skill development a useful starting point to exploring students' development of disciplinary skills over time (see figure 1.1).[2] Disciplinary literacy will require that teacher participants not only learn about work that already exists on the topic, such as the Shanahans' heuristic and more recent research about disciplinary literacy, but also play a role in developing their own new instructional strategies to support the specific needs that arise when their students and their disciplines meet.

During this essential early group learning about disciplinary literacy, participants often experience a sort of apprenticeship exploration. Understanding disciplinary habits and ways of thinking is key for teachers, and it takes some unpacking to help them uncover and name the hidden ways of knowing in their disciplines. We suggest that facilitators encourage participants to consider their own learning in each discipline and how and why they decided to pursue a path in a specific discipline such as history, biology, or music. In addition to uncovering these disciplinary habits of mind, teams should also consider how academic language tends to work across and within disciplines.

In our experience, often, though not always, teachers choose to pursue a discipline that made sense to them as young people, rather than one that was intensely frustrating, and so sometimes the habits of mind within that discipline can be partially hidden. It is genuinely difficult for teachers to *see* the habits of mind and norms of practice within their disciplines if those habits and norms always came naturally. Moreover, this can make it difficult to name and reveal those ways of thinking and working to students, who may not experience the same natural inclination toward particular disciplines. This work of uncovering habits is an important beginning to any disciplinary literacy initiative, because it initiates the complex work of specifying the particular demands of the disciplines and revealing their distinct differences.

For example, many history teachers are naturally inclined toward sourcing and reading for bias, always questioning who wrote a particular document, for what audience, for what purpose, and with what political or ideological slant. Even though history teachers themselves may read this way, many might initially struggle to name these disciplinary habits of mind that have become routine and thus struggle to teach them explicitly to students. Early professional learning for teachers can help them to begin uncovering their own discipline-specific ways of working, in service of making those processes more explicit for students.

Following some initial learning about the broad aims of disciplinary literacy instruction, it can be useful to then review research about why students at the secondary level might still struggle to read and write. Though useful research and practical advice is available on these topics, often teachers in the disciplines have not had opportunities to learn about these struggles, especially in disciplines beyond language arts. Often, content teachers feel the challenges of supporting students who are not reading and writing at the level that is expected for their grade, but they have rarely had opportunities to understand why these struggles are not addressed in earlier grades or how to support students who advance in grades without gaining the skills they need for success. By doing this learning about continued struggle, teacher participants often find new understandings of how students are performing on everyday tasks and how these struggles manifest at times as resistance. This sets the stage for exploring various high-leverage literacy domains that can support student skill development. Consider the shifts in thinking that Julie Padgett, team leader for the math team at Brookline High School (part of the Content-Area Reading Initiative), describes as she and her team emerged from an initial summer institute focused on disciplinary literacy. (See the Snapshot of Practice "Early Learning in a Summer Institute.")

SNAPSHOT OF PRACTICE
Early Learning in a Summer Institute

The Content-Area Reading Initiative (CRI) at Brookline High School fundamentally changed the way that our team thinks about literacy in mathematics. Going into CRI, our team of six math teachers thought that literacy meant reading and writing, both of which we have actively tried to avoid in math. Over the years, we had removed "unnecessary" reading from our activities because we thought it was holding our students back from being able to understand the "math." The summer institute taught us that literacy is far more than just reading and writing—it's communication and comes in many forms that we hadn't considered "literacy," including discussion and multiple representations of data. We also learned that students will do better with the math if we increase the literacy demands in our curriculum rather than trying to remove them.

After completing the summer institute, we embarked on two years' worth of inquiry cycles into various domains of math and literacy instruction. We began with discourse, as we felt it was the most important one in order to set up routines and expectations at the beginning of the year. We found great success in focusing on mathematics discussions, but found that students were having trouble engaging in quality discussions because of a lack of vocabulary understanding, which launched us into an inquiry cycle on vocabulary. We rounded out our first year with a cycle on reading, which took us into our second summer and began our second year. The second year also included cycles on productive failure as a habit of mind and writing in math. Our time together during CRI was some of the best professional development that we've ever done. Some of our biggest takeaways from our work include allowing time for class discussions actually saves time overall because the discussions really work to build student understanding; making word problems relevant to their lives increases student understanding and interest/engagement; and regularly assigning readings and making it part of the routine of a math class makes students engage in the activity and not cringe at having to read outside of English class. At the end of the first year of CRI, I asked my students to reflect on their favorite lesson or topic throughout the year; every single student in all of my classes selected a CRI-based lesson or topic.

The summer institute opened our eyes to the importance of spending more time focusing on literacy, instead of removing it from our curriculum, and it jump-started two great years of work. We left those five days of work together energized and full of ideas about literacy work that we wanted to do together.

~Julie Padgett, Math Teacher and Math Team Leader,
Content-Area Reading Initiative, Brookline High School

A few key adolescent literacy domains

After learning about broad literacy challenges, we have found that there are also a number of high-leverage domains associated with disciplinary literacy that are important to learn about in the early days of an initiative. They are high leverage because they are often of interest to secondary teachers and central to secondary curricula.

Because our framework asks teacher teams to identify topics for inquiry, setting the stage with potential fruitful avenues for exploration is important. Some domains we recommend include (see table 7.1 for more details about each):

- Vocabulary
- Academic language
- Discussion
- Digital literacy
- Use of multiple texts
- Writing to learn

This list is certainly not comprehensive, but these domains are ones teams most often ask us about. As a result, we regularly present on these domains in order to form a strong foundation for teams' more independent inquiries in the future.

In the initial learning phase, it is not necessary to cover every aspect of each disciplinary literacy topic. Instead, we advise the original disciplinary literacy leadership team to select a few of the domains that seem most pertinent

TABLE 7.1   Key domains for early group learning about literacy

Domain	Broad domain overview	Notes on key learning in this domain
Vocabulary	This domain, learning the words needed for doing classwork in various disciplines, includes a focus on the words students read and hear but also the words they are expected to use themselves.	A key to learning in this domain is ensuring that participants explore both highly disciplinary word learning and also explore the more general academic words needed for producing and understanding academic texts.
Academic language	The domain of academic language focuses on the key facets of language beyond the individual word level that contribute to academic discourses.	The facets of language learned in this domain include things like complex syntax with embedded clauses, organization of texts, and cautious and detached stance. Often, participants have not focused on these more connected elements of academic language beyond vocabulary.
Discussion	This domain focuses on how oral communication takes place in classrooms as students discuss opinions, evidence, and thought processes with their peers.	Frequently, learning about discussion is quite different for teachers in different disciplines, as some disciplines require argumentation and persuasion, while others require explication of facts and findings.

(*continued*)

TABLE 7.1　Key domains for early group learning about literacy *(continued)*

Domain	Broad domain overview	Notes on key learning in this domain
Digital literacy	The focus in this domain is on the variety of technological tools students use to read, write, and communicate in classrooms and in their lives outside schools.	This is a very broad focus area, with topics ranging from reading online, to effective incorporation of technology into classrooms, to the impact of social media on students' literacy skills. But effective navigation of the online world of information is a key learning for many groups that focus on this domain.
Use of multiple texts	This domain includes how we use a mix of texts in classrooms to differentiate, scaffold, and support a wide variety of readers in disciplinary classrooms and to supplement key texts in various disciplines.	Key learnings here have to do with using multiple texts with varying levels of scope—from using several long texts in literature circles to using multiple short texts to build background knowledge. But there is always a focus here on how to support students in synthesizing what they learn from an array of texts.
Writing to learn	The focus in this domain is on the variety of everyday writing tasks students use in classrooms to facilitate their learning, such as taking notes, completing graphic organizers, or writing evidence to use in lab reports.	The tasks learned about in this domain are often key sites of learning for the habits of mind emphasized in the disciplines, but students are unlikely to receive much explicit instruction in completing these tasks, unlike the more formal writing tasks of particular subjects. Here, a focus on supporting students in learning these tasks is a key takeaway.

Source: J. Ippolito, J. F. Lawrence, and C. Zaller (eds.), *Getting to the Core of Adolescent Literacy* (Cambridge, MA: Harvard Educational Publishing Group, 2013).

to particular teams, departments, and schools. Once domains have been selected, we tend to use the following guiding questions to help explore any new domain:

- How does knowledge in this domain have an impact on student performance on classroom tasks?
- How do skills in this domain develop over time?

- How might some students need scaffolding around this domain?
- How is knowledge of this domain present in the curriculum or assessments in each discipline?
- What are some basic strategies teachers use to support students' developing skills in this domain?

By delving into these basic questions, often with some initial support from outside experts, teams will, through the course of their discussions and learning, begin to develop a shared vocabulary to use when thinking about literacy in the disciplines. They will begin to unearth areas wherein the disciplines differ and areas in which we want to encourage largely shared practices.

For instance, in an initial learning experience, a team of English teachers and a team of science teachers might both begin to talk about how evidence is used to defend arguments or claims in written responses. The teams might develop a general format for helping students to write "claim-evidence-reasoning" responses to encourage shared language and processes across departments. At the same time, each team might begin to consider what counts as a claim and what kinds of evidence each discipline values—noting and emphasizing disciplinary differences as they tailor the claim-evidence-reasoning writing processes for each discipline. Thus, the teams can start to uncover commonalities and differences among disciplines right from the beginning of the professional learning project.

Additionally, teams will do an important additional task—uncovering fertile ground for later investigation in inquiry cycles (the next step of the professional learning process, explored in chapter 8). We have found that this set of large topics related to disciplinary literacy is both familiar and foreign enough to help teams begin thinking of their own work a bit differently and to both celebrate and reconsider their own current instructional practices. Ultimately, these early topical investigations set the stage nicely for future inquiry. This stage-setting work is highly important; if teams do not want to pursue further inquiry after initial learning, then instructional practice is unlikely to change. Early exploration of these domains can lay the groundwork for teams to work toward identifying inquiry topics they would like to explore; experts or outside consultants can support this process. But teams must also initially learn to collaborate, which we will explore in the next section.

Collaboration next

Learning about literacy is important and fertile ground for beginning a disciplinary literacy initiative. But, there is often more that teams must learn in order to effectively begin working together. In some school contexts, especially at the high school level, teachers have rarely been expected to work collaboratively. Sometimes teachers come together in groups or departments to take care of logistical business, but teachers working in teams to attend to problems of practice are less common. And even if they have worked together previously, new teams must find their own ways to collaborate.

Collaboration requires some early learning about tools to become more effective and efficient. Merely having time to work together will not result in a highly effective team. Instead, each team must learn to collaborate as a group in a way that makes teaching practice public and sets them up to inquire together about topics of interest in their particular school settings. Early training in collaborative work, with a brief review of associated collaborative learning tools, can help establish this orientation as a habit for teams to adopt (see table 7.2 for a description of some collaborative learning domains that are important to review early in a professional learning project, to help teams organize themselves for success).

Early on, teams and team members, especially those within large schools, may need support in getting to know each other and establishing early understandings about one another's work preferences, including building norms for shared work. It might seem unusual to do this sort of work with teachers who already work together in the same department, school, or district, but in our experience, even teachers who have worked together for a long time still have much to learn about each other's work preferences and classrooms. Because of the traditionally autonomous nature of teaching, colleagues may know each other personally while still knowing very little about how they prefer to work or the specifics of how they run their own classrooms.[3] For team members to work together successfully, they must get past this unfamiliarity and begin building a shared sense of mission and working style.

Additionally, at the start of any initiative, it is important to explore tools that help teams collaborate. Specifically, we have found that discussion-based protocols help organize and clarify discussions and ensure all participants are

TABLE 7.2   Key domains for early group learning about collaboration

Domain	Broad domain overview	Notes on key learning in this domain
Team building	In this domain, teams come together to get to know one another and begin recognizing the strengths each person brings to the team.	Often, especially on high school teams, participants may not have had many opportunities to collaborate. In these cases, team-building time is particularly well spent.
Collaborative norms	It is important early in an initiative for groups to begin considering how they function best as a group and how to meet different individual needs across the team.	There are typically team members who value different sorts of progress in working together. Some value focusing on processes, and others feel accomplished when they create products. It is important to understand these differences.
Protocols	In this area, teams will begin to explore and use a number of discussion-based protocols to help guide their discussions and to help identify early inquiry topics.	We recommend using a variety of discussion-based protocols to structure discussions and to carry those discussions to logical endpoints.
Work structures	During the early group learning phase, team leaders will begin helping their teams identify structures for moving ahead and which structures work particularly well or seem interesting to the team.	Groups might choose early in the work to begin by doing some reading, assessment, looking at student work or curriculum, or consulting other resources.
Making practice public	One key and sometimes stressful element of this early group learning is to begin helping teachers support each other to make their practices more public to each other.	By supporting teams during early group learning as they begin to share their own curriculum, lesson plans, and ideas, teams will begin to make public their day-to-day practices and routines, which will be explored later in the project in more depth.

heard. These tools are designed to ensure that discussions lead to logical ending points, rather than meandering without moving the group's goals forward. In early group learning, team leaders need to have a chance to learn about some useful protocols to help guide inquiry with their teams and practice using those protocols, ideally with guidance and feedback from experts, to lead their teams in early discussions as literacy learning is taking place. Team leaders can then begin leading their teams as they process initial learning, ensuring that when they ultimately begin to work independently, each team will have an early collaborative foundation upon which to build.

THE STRUCTURE OF EARLY GROUP LEARNING

In our experience, early group learning takes different shapes, depending on school context. But early group learning, we have found, works best when it includes some choice between a few common components of professional learning. We have seen various approaches be successful if well matched to the context. Three common structures that teams have used to begin their initial learning are as follows:

- **An opening institute, often held during summer.** Many successful initiatives have begun with some dedicated workshop time together; groups we have worked with have spent anywhere from two to five days together studying the topics described earlier, most often under the guidance of consultants, experts, or facilitators with some expertise in the field. This institute is perhaps the most common and successful way we have seen schools open an initiative, though it is not always possible in every context.
- **An opening book (or other text) study.** Some initiatives have begun with the team studying a common text or set of materials together, similar to a book group, to set the stage for learning. A handful of texts and online materials lend themselves nicely to this sort of initial exploration (See the appendix, "Recommended Reading for Beginning with a Text Study," at the end of this chapter for recommendations).
- **Daylong professional learning sessions spread throughout the year.** At some schools, teachers are unable to find time over summer to start learning together, so some projects begin during the year with standalone professional development sessions spread out across weeks and months. This approach tends to result in a slightly slower launch than the others, but sometimes it is the only logistical one that makes sense for a particular school.

Next we will describe each of these potential structures in a bit more depth, and we provide some general lessons learned from many experiences with early group learning.

If you choose to implement an opening institute, which is the pathway we most highly recommend, consider who will present information about literacy to the group without placing the burden of preparing this presentation on team members. Often, outside consultants who are literacy experts, or individuals within a school or district—instructional leaders, specialists, coaches, or teachers with literacy training and facilitative expertise—can do this work. These facilitative leaders can present some of the literacy domains to teams, and team leaders can take a leadership role in helping teams process this new learning and connect it to their own classroom work.

Choosing to open with a text study operates slightly differently from the other approaches, but it can be a cost-effective way to support teams in getting started. Choosing to work with a text that covers some of the key topics in disciplinary literacy and then coming together to process that text can also set the stage to begin a collaborative initiative. In this model, however, it can be a challenge to ensure that all participants will have the time or motivation to engage with the text prior to coming together to share. Building in some meeting time during which participants can explore the text, if there is concern about participants finding time to read independently, can be helpful.

Opening with professional learning days spread across a school year is another approach that some schools undertake, especially when they are unable to find a way to begin during the summer. Though these projects often result in some excellent learning for participants, starting with days embedded in the school year often means teams take longer to begin their collaborative work and typically make progress at a slower pace than teams that begin during the summer. We recommend, if at all possible, that design teams try to carve out time outside the school year to start the early learning work that sets the stage for further learning. Consider the various ways of beginning, coming together, and learning over time that occurred in the Snapshot of Practice "Multiple Paths to Success in Collaborative Learning," from Brooke Feldman of the One Dorchester project in Boston, a collaborative learning initiative that brought together teachers from three different schools (private, public, and charter).

SNAPSHOT OF PRACTICE
Multiple Paths to Success in Collaborative Learning

The One Dorchester project brought together teachers from the Jeremiah Burke High School, Boston Collegiate Charter School, and Cristo Rey Boston. This initiative created the nation's first professional learning community comprising teachers from district, charter, and independent schools. I was fortunate to participate in and lead OneDot's social studies team from 2013 to 2015.

Our group consisted of early and mid-career teachers with degrees in social studies education, history, and political science. In spite of our many years of undergraduate and graduate training, we realized that we had to learn more about literacy instruction in order to meet the needs of the diverse learners in our classrooms. We started by reading *Building Students' Historical Literacies: Learning to Read and Reason with Historical Texts and Evidence* by Jeffrey Nokes. Our conversations focused on how we could use his theories and research in our classrooms.

We realized, however, that we needed more direct instruction to maximize our impact on students' learning. Fortunately, we were able to convene a OneDot literacy conference in the summer of 2014. (The OneDot physics team reached a similar conclusion; the teachers needed more professional development on disciplinary literacy.) In our three-day workshop, we learned how to help students forge identities as readers, decipher between independent and instructional reading levels, and analyze the relationships between text, task, reader, and environment.

This workshop propelled our team's learning and teaching. We embraced the work of Sam Wineburg and the Stanford History Education Group, and we started to focus on how we could help students become better historical readers, writers, thinkers, speakers, and creators. We used our new learning to craft lessons and create common assessments. We also used it as a foundation to observe each other's teaching and provide targeted feedback on our literacy instruction.

Without a doubt, the work on disciplinary literacy has transformed the trajectory of my career. Since OneDot, I have transitioned from classroom teacher to curriculum coordinator. In this role, I support, coach, and supervise a team of fifteen middle school social studies teachers. I help my teachers understand the importance of literacy in the social studies classroom and share with them the tools, strategies, and resources I have learned.

In a recent department meeting, we discussed how contextualization can be a key to unlocking misconceptions. Students often view primary sources as stagnant, or they wrestle with presentism. However, orienting a source in its dynamic time and place can help students understand the author's perspective, motivations, and intended audience. In this workshop, we brainstormed strategies to introduce, frame, or review historical context as way to help increase reading comprehension. A few days later, a veteran teacher enthusiastically reported that, after using one of the strategies, his students truly understood the complex source he challenged them to read. And he plans to focus more on how he can use disciplinary literacy tools to help his students make sense of the past.

> ~Brooke Feldman, History Teacher and Social Studies Team Leader,
> OneDot Project, Boston Collegiate Charter School

DIFFERENT PATHWAYS FOR DIFFERENT TEAMS

Different projects will begin their work in different ways, and each literacy leadership design team must tailor the beginning of a project to best suit the needs of its school context. Smart decisions early in the work can get a project off to a meaningful start and lead to productive collaboration. This is not to say that every project should begin in precisely the same way. Different teams might use different structures, or they might focus on different domains depending on what past professional learning initiatives have covered or which needs have been identified. These decisions can be governed by logistical concerns, but more importantly, they should rely on and draw from the needs analysis done by the design team in the early planning stages of the project.

Occasionally, we have worked on projects that have not been able to begin with an early group learning experience. Sometimes finances or scheduling can make it difficult for groups to find time to work together early on, and these projects have gone on to do some good work through inquiry. But, it often takes much longer for these teams to begin to work together effectively, and they have often backtracked to make some group learning space later in the project after they struggle to get momentum going. So, we recommend that groups structure their work to begin in this way, even if they are unable to find as much time together as they might like.

A few suggested practices, no matter how a project begins

Over time, working with a variety of different sites and contexts, we have learned a few lessons about maximizing opportunities as professional learning projects begin. Design teams might consider the following suggestions as they think about how to support early group learning:

- **Make space to turn off day-to-day operations.** We often suggest conducting early group learning *before* the school year begins, because participants find it challenging to turn off the everyday business of the school year once students arrive back at school. But a summer institute is not the only way to ensure that teachers are able to focus on new learning; we have seen projects successfully use professional learning days off-site or otherwise manage to create space in their own buildings for teachers to engage this new work. Teachers are rightly caught up in an unceasing tide of everyday work that can be hard to set aside in the interest of making space for new learning. Finding ways to create that space to learn new information will always be key to an initiative's success, but never more so than at the project's beginning.
- **Use summer well, at the beginning and beyond, to position teams for success during the year.** Teams that work smart during summer are often able to make more headway in their work together because of the opportunity afforded by being away from the everyday hustle and bustle of a school year. Groups that use time during the summer to do their early group learning with consultants or on their own often create greater momentum and investment early in a project, because they have time to plan together before the year's curriculum begins. This progress can continue with work during subsequent summers. We know that not all districts have the time and resources for this summer structure, but we suggest it whenever it is feasible.
- **Strike a balance between being led by text, in-person experts, and teacher leaders.** A project may begin with consultants' or authors' presentations, but expertise about the school context, the curriculum, and the students will always reside within the teams themselves. In this way, team leaders should help lead participants through making these connections and exploring their own context in more depth. This situates the work of the project within the teams, rather than within individuals who are not part of the teams.

- **Remember that team building is time well spent.** It can be easy to feel as though every moment of time together must be spent actively in pursuit of new knowledge about literacy, but spending time working on building teams, getting to know each other's work styles, and learning to work effectively together is worthwhile in the long run. Teams that neglect to do this sort of work early in a project often experience difficulty navigating conflict or maintaining momentum once inquiry work gets underway.
- **Consistently encourage connection to the particulars of the site and its classrooms.** Often, in traditional professional development workshops, a key issue is that participants are passive. But by setting up many situations throughout the early learning wherein team leaders can ask participants to make connections between new learning and current classroom practice, teachers are able to begin identifying their own students' strengths and weaknesses and narrowing the field for future inquiry.
- **Try to avoid focusing too much on what is not changeable.** Teachers commonly experience some level of frustration about the day-to-day business of school operations or the reality of teaching students with many needs, and sometimes frustrations like these can make their way into group learning. But a disciplinary literacy initiative rarely can help with issues such as a clearer schedule or a better system for dealing with behavioral issues. Therefore, facilitators must keep the focus on the project at hand and what *can* be changed and improved through a disciplinary literacy initiative.
- **Remind participants that collaborative learning projects are not about easy answers, but about group discovery and invention of instructional improvements across time.** Often, when entering into an initiative, teachers expect that they will be presented with answers to solve literacy issues quickly in their classrooms. In the case of disciplinary literacy though, the process will be one of inquiry and trial and error over time. Helping participants understand this will be a key to helping them clarify their expectations for what will happen as the project gets underway.

We do not mean our advice about early group learning in this chapter to be prescriptive, but rather reflective of our own experiences guiding disciplinary literacy professional learning initiatives and our best synthesis about what is known about professional learning. Because literacy in the disciplines is a unique and complex challenge, creating spaces for teams of teachers to begin their work of improving literacy instruction is vital.

Design and leadership teams should carefully consider how their groups will work and allow team leaders to begin the work of investigating literacy practices in their own contexts and disciplines. By setting the stage with effective early group learning, we create spaces for the inquiry work that teams will do to implement, adapt, and invent new instructional practices to support disciplinary literacy.

APPENDIX (Chapter 7)

Recommended Reading for Beginning with a Text Study

- *Reading and Writing in the Disciplines.* This online module, available from Annenberg Learner, introduces disciplinary literacy and how literacy differs in four disciplines: math, science, social studies, and English/language arts. It is available at https://www.learner.org/courses/readwrite/index.html.

- *Developing Readers in the Academic Disciplines*, by Doug Buehl (Newark, DE: International Reading Association, 2011). This user-friendly title is a clear introduction to disciplinary literacy and provides great examples from classrooms and content areas.

- *Building Academic Language: Meeting Common Core Standards Across Disciplines, Grades 5–12* (2nd ed.), by Jeff Zwiers (San Francisco: John Wiley, 2014). This title introduces how language functions differently from discipline to discipline; it contains great examples across middle and high school classrooms.

- *Adolescent Literacy in the Era of the Common Core: From Research into Practice*, eds. Jacy Ippolito, Joshua Fahey Lawrence, and Colleen Zaller (Cambridge, MA: Harvard Education Press, 2013). This volume focuses on introducing research and practice about literacy domains related to disciplinary literacy, such as vocabulary, digital literacy, or the use of multiple texts, often introduced to teachers early in a disciplinary literacy project.

- *Literacy in the Disciplines: A Teacher's Guide for Grades 5–12*, by Thomas DeVere Wolsey and Diane Lapp (New York: Guilford Press, 2016). This user-friendly and practical resource presents excellent information about adult disciplinary experts, as well as strong instructional recommendations.

CHAPTER 8

Collaboratively Inquiring into Domains of Disciplinary Literacy Practice

ONCE TEACHER TEAMS have gained foundational knowledge about disciplinary literacy domains, they are ready to dig into the work of making meaning of those instructional practices and working to make the practices meaningful within their own disciplinary and classroom contexts, which is the fifth step in our framework. Too often, teachers encounter new ideas through single-session professional development sessions, often attended by teachers from many schools and districts, meaning the work is sometimes divorced from context. This can make it difficult to focus on context-specific, adaptive challenges such as exploring disciplinary literacy. If we know that context-specific learning over time is the best mechanism for truly having an impact on teacher instructional practice, then one-off, context-divorced professional learning experiences are unlikely to encourage deep disciplinary literacy explorations. Instead, when teams of teachers work together within a content-specific or cross-content area team to integrate new literacy strategies into their practice, they benefit greatly from ongoing collegial insight. Colleagues who know and understand a particular school context and its students can help each other to move from understanding ideas about disciplinary literacy to enacting disciplinary literacy practices. We believe that the practice of shared inquiry–in the form of *inquiry cycles*–provides the meaningful structures and processes for teams to work together, digging into how best to develop tailored disciplinary literacy strategies for their students.

An inquiry cycle is a process by which each teacher team within a disciplinary literacy professional learning project might focus for a while on a mutually agreed-upon question or topic. There is some variety in how inquiry cycles might look based on how initiatives are structured and how school contexts organize teachers into groups; in this chapter, we describe the basic shape of a traditional inquiry cycle. First, we provide a brief overview of each step in the inquiry cycle process, and in subsequent chapters, we dive more deeply into the processes involved in some of these steps. We start by explaining why adopting an inquiry stance is so critical within disciplinary literacy professional learning projects.

WHY INQUIRY?

Teacher inquiry recognizes the expertise and important ideas that teachers themselves hold, as well as the potential for the development of effective new ideas within and among groups of teachers (see chapter 2). Marilyn Cochran-Smith and Susan Lytle point to inquiry as a practice that holds great potential to generate ideas that, in turn, lead to changes in teacher practice.[1] Notably, inquiry leads not only to new ideas that can affect instructional practice, but also to improved working relationships among those inquiring together in a group or on a team. Working together, as Cochran-Smith and Lytle note, teams of teachers are likely to generate important insights and new approaches to teaching while also nurturing these important collaborative relationships. As such, we believe it is an ideal component of disciplinary literacy professional learning initiatives.

An inquiry approach to professional learning also signals that learning is a lifelong process. Learning about a particular new approach to instruction–such as disciplinary literacy–often does not fit easily into a discrete time frame. Instead, in the case of disciplinary literacy professional learning, as teachers work with new ideas, new questions naturally emerge, and adopting an inquiry approach allows teachers to bring those questions to the table. Joining together in inquiry with colleagues means that new ideas are jointly constructed, with questions that one team member brings to the group often being answered by a colleague, as opposed to waiting to talk to an external expert or searching for an answer elsewhere.

This is not to devalue the importance of outside expertise at critical points in the inquiry process. For instance, in the learning process we outline in this book, we suggest that teachers initially learn important information about disciplinary literacy from up-front, intensive learning opportunities such as summer institutes. Teacher teams can then use this early group learning to spur inquiry cycles. In this way, teachers can integrate new knowledge from summer institutes with their own team's shared knowledge of discipline-specific best practices, focusing their inquiry on how best to apply this newly integrated knowledge into their teaching practice. Ultimately, this allows teams to quickly synthesize and apply new learning in an active and collaborative manner.

One example of an inquiry cycle comes from Brookline High School's Content-Area Reading Initiative math team, which learned in its summer institute about the power of rich, open-ended academic discussions in middle and high school math classrooms. After reviewing a handful of high-leverage, research-based "talk moves" (e.g., revoicing, restating, prompting, and so on) in the initial summer institute, the math team began its school year with the inquiry question, "What difference might it make in students' mathematical reasoning if we introduced and practiced more mathematically focused academic discussions?" The team spent roughly two months documenting what happened as each team member intentionally introduced and used academic talk moves in their classroom. The teachers shared lesson plans, observed one another, videotaped their classes, and reviewed the footage to learn which talk moves were most successful at getting students to use mathematical terminology and to explain their problem solving and reasoning to one another. The knowledge generated through this process, by the group and its inquiry, was more meaningful and responsive to student needs than anything an individual teacher might have gained at an outside workshop or working with these concepts independently. By the end of its first inquiry cycle, the team had generated a number of thoughtful ways in which focusing on academically productive talk did, in fact, seem to increase students' mathematical reasoning—the beginning of their professional learning work around disciplinary literacy.

OVERVIEW OF INQUIRY CYCLE STEPS

Next we review in more detail the various steps within a traditional disciplinary literacy inquiry cycle: defining a question or topic, building background knowledge, collaboratively generating ideas, individually testing ideas, and sharing and revising ideas and practices.

While teacher inquiry structures are certainly not new, we find that disciplinary literacy professional learning projects must devote some time to helping teams of teachers define, structure, and engage in focused inquiry cycles. The steps shown in figure 2.2 are what we have typically outlined for teams interested in engaging in inquiry together over time.

Defining an inquiry question or topic

First, teams must work to define a disciplinary literacy question or focus. While this sounds simple, crafting an effective question (not too broad, not too narrow, focused on both literacy and content goals, allowing all team members to find an entry point into the conversation) can be quite challenging. One of the reasons we often suggest that disciplinary literacy professional learning projects begin with a summer institute, or some other form of intensive group learning, is so that teams might begin their work with a rich trove of possible inquiry topics and a shared language for discussing those possible topics. It is often best to end such a summer institute with opportunities for teams to discuss possible inquiry topics, each of which may be later explored for weeks or even months.

Often, teachers use classroom or school-level data to inform decision making around a focal topic. The inquiry topic might come in the form of a question: how might we better teach vocabulary and integrate word study into our daily science instruction? Or, it might come in the form of a concept: we hope to investigate the concept of text sets and how to use them in a foreign language classroom. The purpose of using inquiry as a component of this professional learning framework is to build ongoing learning into the overall professional learning initiative. Through coming together, teams will inevitably deepen and revise their knowledge about their focal topic.

Building background knowledge and drawing on experts

Next, teams might seek to build their background knowledge around a specific disciplinary literacy topic, drawing on early intensive learning (e.g., a summer institute) and seeking out new information to help them address the question that frames their inquiry. Expert knowledge is an important foundational component of inquiry. Teams will build on the knowledge acquired from disciplinary literacy experts, but this process does not follow the traditional professional development trajectory. In traditional professional development settings, the assumption is often that experts will deliver knowledge that teachers will take up and then immediately implement with little alteration. In contrast, our framework of professional learning foregrounds teacher expertise, adaptation, and invention.

In practice, this means that teams of teachers will take up the initial information shared by disciplinary literacy experts (whether in the form of knowledge shared directly through seminars and workshops or more indirectly through readings and texts on the topic) and then use that information in a generative manner to spur their own inquiry, invention, integration, application, and assessment processes. By building on initial ideas from experts, teams of teachers then grapple together with how the ideas apply to their particular discipline, classrooms, and students. In this sense, teachers filter and process expert knowledge, taking into consideration the details of particular school and classroom contexts. So, the math team mentioned earlier, which was focusing on discussion and teacher talk moves, might read research about discussion and academic language to see what experts know about best practices in facilitating authentic, meaningful classroom conversations both generally and in math classrooms specifically. This process of drawing on expertise from the field and combining it with teacher expertise about particular class contexts and disciplines is a foundational component of the inquiry process.

Collaborative idea generation

At the heart of the inquiry process lies the work of teachers grappling with newly learned concepts in disciplinary literacy and then developing new teaching approaches that integrate these ideas into their work. This process of collaborative idea generation, which takes place in disciplinary or cross-disciplinary teams, represents the meat of the inquiry process. Teachers might then use a newly learned approach related to disciplinary literacy and spin off ideas for revising that idea for their particular students or given their particular curriculum. Teams might also start their work by applying ideas learned from intensive summer institutes or from the literature in their particular disciplinary classrooms in order to form a foundation for further idea generation together, based on the outcome of enacting those practices. Or, team members might consider what a particular disciplinary literacy concept, such as the use of discussion, means for their particular discipline (e.g., "What does discussion look like in a math classroom?").

The work of idea generation can be messy, and it needs time. For instance, if a team of science teachers comes together, guided by a question about what role vocabulary development can play in their science classrooms, they may require an entire weekly meeting just to agree about which types of vocabulary words (and word parts) might be important to explicitly teach in various science classes such as biology, chemistry, or physics. Then, they might spend two or three meetings brainstorming various ways to integrate vocabulary instruction into their respective classes. In order to bring the ideas to life, they could sketch out the details of a lesson or two. Or they could create two different versions of a similar lesson, with two teachers agreeing to each teach one version.

Depending on each team's learning preferences, the pace of the inquiry process—idea generation, testing, and reflection—will naturally vary. Additionally, the topic the team is exploring, curriculum mandates at the school or district level, the population of students served, and the demands of the school year will also contribute to the pace of any given team inquiry. Thus, flexibility around timing is key, and team leaders can read their teams and recommend when to speed up or slow down as needed to keep the inquiry process moving forward at a reasonable rate.

The work of collaborative idea generation embodies the nonlinear nature of inquiry. Also, it positions the members of each inquiry team as the *real* experts. Building on knowledge gained from experts in the field, team members can develop new ideas through careful (sometimes slow) consideration, debate, and deliberation, relying on their knowledge of their own students and school context to shape meaningful, relevant ideas and practices. We see this illustrated in special educator Brenna Mahoney's Snapshot of Practice, "Early Inquiry and Idea Generation," which details her work on a team focused on support services at the high school level.

SNAPSHOT OF PRACTICE
Early Inquiry and Idea Generation

For two years, a team of six Brookline High School educators researched the use of multitiered systems of support (MTSS) at the secondary level. We coined ourselves the "Hybrid Team" due to our broad range of educational backgrounds. Our team was made up of two content teachers, a special educator, a speech and language pathologist, a reading specialist, and the leader of our tutorial program (which is a general education academic support program). The Hybrid Team spent two years together. We shared a mission of finding ways to better support our struggling students, but we didn't know what those supports were or how to identify those students. So, we began our inquiry work with the simple intention of putting ourselves in our struggling students' shoes. Using a reading assessment developed and administered by our colleagues in the social studies department, we identified a tenth grader in college preparatory courses who was struggling with reading comprehension, both inferential and fact based.

Each member of the team shadowed her throughout one day. Later, when we all shared our separate observations, we were struck by how stressed the student appeared in all her classes. When her English teacher asked her to read aloud, she squirmed and attempted to refuse. When her history teacher asked her a text-based question about an article they had just read, she lowered her head and said, "I don't know." This experience helped us better understand the negative behaviors (e.g., avoidance, shutting down, defiance) we see daily, and how they may be closely correlated to students' academic weaknesses. This experience invigorated us as we began our next steps. Even though our mission was to change our school's systems of supports, we realized we needed to practice implementing these interventions in our own classrooms first. Throughout the first year, we engaged in a variety of inquiry cycles including questioning, inferencing, and active reading strategies. This trial and error in the safety of our own classrooms gave us the confidence to return to our original goal of developing a more systematic approach to interventions at the secondary level.

~Brenna Mahoney, Special Education Teacher,
    Content-Area Reading Initiative, Brookline High School

As is evident in this snapshot, the Hybrid Team collaboratively decided to shadow a struggling reader in order to learn more about adolescents' experiences across classes and content areas. Their observations, and subsequent group reflections, generated an entire year's worth of further investigations into reading, writing, and communication strategies related to questioning, inferencing, and active reading. Ultimately, it was their early idea generation (brainstorming about how observations could help them better understand students' experiences) that led to rich inquiry work throughout the year. (See the box "Questions Teams Might Ask During Collaborative Idea Generation.")

QUESTIONS TEAMS MIGHT ASK DURING COLLABORATIVE IDEA GENERATION

- Given our inquiry focus, how might this look in my classroom, given my subject and my students?
- What are our goals for our students (in our discipline) related to a particular domain of disciplinary literacy? (e.g., what are our goals for our history students related to reading historical texts?)
- How might we break down a disciplinary literacy domain into manageable content and procedural chunks that we could then begin to take on in our classrooms?
- What might we need to shift about the design of our courses in order to address a particular disciplinary literacy domain?
- Who on our team might already be doing some of the work of addressing a particular disciplinary literacy domain such that we might observe them in order to spark further ideas?
- What is one practice we might all commit to trying in order to start shifting our teaching in a particular literacy domain?

Idea generation can be messy, and in these cases, figuring out who is guiding the work can be important. When teams work together to generate new ideas for how best to integrate disciplinary literacy practices into their instruction, the work can get messy, confusing, and even contentious. Given that, it is vital to bring some structure to the work. As noted in chapters 5 and 6, many successful teams designate a teacher leader to guide the work. One can imagine, in the midst of whirling conversations about how best to shape a new disciplinary literacy instructional approach that, without structure and boundaries and guidance, the conversation could run amok. When teams are in the midst of inquiry, team leaders often need to provide some guidance and structure to group conversations. Over time, we have found that team leaders are particularly effective at providing guidance for inquiry by doing some of the following:

- Choosing among protocols to help provide structure to idea generation conversations. Some of the best protocols can be found on the School Reform Initiative website, http://www.schoolreforminitiative.org/protocols/
- Helping a team to choose a single, narrow focus to guide inquiry over a span of time
- Outlining various roles within the group that can facilitate effective conversations, such as timekeeper, note taker, and so on
- Listening for the ideas that emerge in the midst of conversation and moving those ideas forward in the conversation
- Discerning when a particular inquiry cycle might have run its course and suggesting that the team develop a new inquiry focus
- Checking in with team members individually in order to see how they are translating ideas that emerge within the group into their individual practice
- Connecting with experts in the field in order to gather resources that might forward a particular inquiry focus

Individual idea testing

Once team members have developed a number of approaches for integrating new disciplinary literacy practices into their teaching, it is time for teachers to go back to their classrooms in order to test out the ideas. Though this work often happens individually, it is an essential component of the team-based inquiry process. So, the math team we have been describing that is focused on discussion might identify a few practices each member wants to try and when they will each integrate these strategies into their respective classrooms to see how they work and how students respond.

In some cases, each member of a team tests out the same idea. In others, we have found that teams prefer to have one member test out an idea and then report back to the whole group. Finally, on some teams, each member tests out a different version of a particular new instructional idea. There is no one right way to go about the idea-testing process. For some teams, this process is quite organic, with different team members testing out either the same or slightly different ideas as it works for them, over the course of a few weeks, and chiming in with feedback for the group when they are able.

Idea testing is a vital component of the inquiry process not because it is an opportunity to prove that the ideas the group generated were revolutionary or perfectly formed. Instead, idea testing provides the necessary data for reflective conversations about the ideas–conversations that will inevitably lead to the revision and sharpening of new and more effective approaches to disciplinary literacy instruction. Idea testing can be seen as a process intended to generate data. Whether the ideas prove wildly successful or fall flat is less important. Instead, when a teacher engages in idea testing, bringing data about those tests back to the rest of the team is the most important step. These data could be in the form of student work, a video of teaching practice, handouts shared with a class, or just a narrative about a particular lesson. Sharing the process and results of idea testing forms the foundation for the next step of the inquiry cycle, which we can see in the Snapshot of Practice "Idea Testing," by Philip Pietrangelo, an environmental science teacher at a small school in Boston.

SNAPSHOT OF PRACTICE
Idea Testing

Authentically assessing student content knowledge in science can be challenging when literacy and math skills are prerequisites to demonstrating understanding. In the Boston Public Schools, where student progress in the sciences is often stunted by low literacy and math skills, this has become increasingly challenging.

During the 2014–2105 school year, I was privileged to work with a team of pedagogical innovators that realized the potential of an underperforming, and frankly marginalized, population of students. Historical testing data indicated that our students lacked fundamental literacy skills, and the tenth-grade statewide test was looming large on our horizon.

As a response, our grade-level team, with support from our administrators and Christina Dobbs, designed an interdisciplinary and interventionist curriculum with a focus on "deeper understanding" to support literacy skill acquisition. My role, specifically, was to design curriculum and assessment around literacy strategies that would support language acquisition and reading comprehension, as well as collaborating on choosing texts that would work in both science and literacy classes. We settled on the food system as the common ground to develop deep understanding, and I chose to pursue evidence-based argument as a method for demonstrating comprehension.

For the remainder of the year, I replaced traditional testing with projects, presentations, and seminars. My goal was to engage students with scientific texts through discussion, writing, reading, and listening. I borrowed past MCAS [the state test] questions for reading comprehension as a model for writing food system questions. I revised questioning to be less mechanistic and more critical, to be framed around discernment and inference. A sample question included: "What evidence do the authors provide to support their claim, and why does this evidence support that claim?" When students provided weak or anecdotal responses, I was often obliged to tell them I was "unmoved" or "unconvinced" by their answer. A further discussion, and usually a better response demonstrating deeper understanding (or questioning), often ensued. I asked students to "sound like a scientist" on multiple occasions to establish a mind-set for developing an argument. At two points in the spring semester, students showcased their skills during Socratic seminars where "sounding scientific" was a primary objective. Students needed to voice their ideas and formulate evidence-based arguments that required practicing and demonstrating literacy skills, but also critiquing each other's literacy skills with counterarguments or critical responses. I was pleasantly surprised by their willingness to argue, and the stage was set for science to happen organically.

This transformative experience has helped me be better able to address the literacy needs of my students. I cannot say enough about the administrative "space" we were given to explore and decide what was best for our students. I hope that more schools and administrators give teachers this space in order to innovate and collaborate with meaning, purpose, and a shared vision.

~Philip Pietrangelo, *Environmental Science Teacher,*
Tenth-Grade Improvement Project, Boston Green Academy

As Philip suggests in the snapshot of his team's work around scientific literacy, testing a variety of ideas in his own classroom (always in consultation with his team) led to a wide array of changed practices. From a greater focus on evidence-based arguments in discussions and writing, to new discussion structures, to a clearer focus on adopting and using scientific habits of mind, each of these practices was implemented as part of the idea-testing phases of ongoing inquiry throughout the school year. However, these new practices might not have remained in place if it were not for the subsequent shared reflection and idea revision work that occurred back with his team.

Shared reflection and idea revision

While idea testing is generally an individualized process, the data analysis and reflection that follow idea testing are necessarily collaborative. Once back with their team, those who tested out new instructional ideas share the data from those tests with the group. Note, of course, that data in this case can refer to a wide variety of formal and informal pieces of information, from test results to anecdotal teacher notes to student writing samples. Each teacher and team will decide on the right types and amount of data to use as part of their analytic and reflection processes. In reflecting on the data, the team can consider how effective the tested instructional approach was in helping students to develop disciplinary literacy skills. Teachers might look for ways to improve upon the approach tried by one or more group members. In other cases, the group might consider how to merge a number of different approaches in order to better teach a disciplinary literacy skill or strategy. In still other instances, the group might consider what to do next. Given that developing disciplinary literacy skills takes time, a team might agree that instead of revising its approach to a lesson that was taught, its time would be better spent focusing on next steps and thus figuring out what to teach next in order to help students to continue to grow their disciplinary literacy skills.

One of the math teachers highlighted earlier might attempt new discussion instructional activities, such as collaborative Frayer models (see http://www. adlit.org/strategies/22369/ for an example), designed to help students talk to make deeper sense of words and discern relationships between them. Then the teacher would bring the students' work back to the group in order to start a discussion about the strategy's effectiveness, as well as to reflect on the impact on students and the curriculum when the strategy is included. The team might decide whether the strategy is improving student vocabulary use later on other tasks, as well as take up questions such as whether the strategy was difficult to implement or whether to adjust the implementation approach in one way or another.

The inquiry cycle at the heart of our professional learning model is purposefully cyclical. Thus, revision is a key component of the process. Implicitly, this means that failure is also inherent in the process. In some cases, team members might return from the idea-testing stage only to report that an approach to teaching a new disciplinary literacy skill was a complete flop. Failure in cases like this can become rich fodder for conversation within the team, allowing members to generate new approaches based on what did not work for a particular teacher.

Inevitably, the reflection and revision process within a cycle of inquiry leads groups to further hone or shift their focus. So, our group that was initially focused on discussion in math classrooms might realize that what they are really interested in is how students can justify their reasoning for particular choices as they talk with each other. This process of revision–from an initial idea to one that takes a slightly different tack is an expected and important part of the inquiry cycle. Once teams revise their focus or their ideas, they can cycle back through each stage of the inquiry process. Or, teams might revise their instructional ideas slightly and move back into the idea-testing stage, from which they will then quickly return to idea reflection and revision. Team leaders play an important role in this process, helping teams to discern which stage of the inquiry cycle is next for them, once they have moved through one complete cycle. And ultimately, team leaders will also pay close attention to when a team has engaged in a cycle thoroughly and is ready to move on to an entirely new inquiry focus.

In the next chapters, we will explore the process of piloting and assessing new disciplinary literacy instructional practices, as well as sharing and disseminating those practices more widely within a department or school. We will provide tips on how to navigate those stages of the professional learning process, and on how teacher leaders can help teams maintain momentum and make decisions about when to move from one inquiry cycle to the next.

CHAPTER 9

Designing, Testing, and Assessing New Disciplinary Literacy Practices

IN THIS CHAPTER, we illustrate the sixth step in our seven-step professional learning framework, idea testing and shared reflection, in greater detail, as it is perhaps the most challenging part of the overall process. The transition from learning about practices to finding ways to implement them is perhaps the most critical work of disciplinary literacy professional learning initiatives. It is also the stage at which many professional learning projects fail, as teachers learn about new practices but are unable to make the jump to implement them in the midst of crowded curricula and busy school years. In order to avoid this potential sink-hole, we begin with suggestions about how best to frame the transition from exploration to implementation.

POTENTIAL BARRIERS TO INSTRUCTIONAL CHANGE

When implementing new instructional practices, a key is for teacher teams to move from the learning stage into the trial-and-error stage of doing this work, a phase that can feel fraught with risks and uncertainty. In our experience working in various contexts, we often find that teachers feel immense pressure to

139

raise student achievement and, in particular, test scores as an immediate result of professional learning. This urgency to improve is good, but it can also make decisions about new instructional practices feel laden with pressure.

Additionally, implementing new instructional practices and sharing them with others can be scary for teachers who rely heavily on particular routines, those who have had little experience making their practices public, or even those with more experience who have not made changes recently. Planning for this transition into public practice is an important part of making a disciplinary literacy initiative a success, and the structures of PLCs, teacher leaders, and inquiry are designed to support this transition effectively. These structures are important to ensuring that participants feel supported.

Knowing that the process of incorporating new practices into instruction can vary depending on the participant is also critical. Some teachers will experience learning about new literacy domains as exciting and will begin implementing new teaching ideas immediately. Other participants are much more measured in their planning. In response to group learning, some teachers hold off on immediate implementation and changes in practice; instead, they focus on planning for future integration of new strategies into the curriculum. We think of this varying pace of implementation as a normal part of the work, but it can be challenging for team leaders, and even sometimes participants, to understand that every teacher might not implement new practices at the same pace and rate.

CREATING A SPACE TO TINKER BY RELYING ON THE STRUCTURE

If teachers are truly doing their own inquiry work into disciplinary literacy, there is a chance they will be working to improve student skills in areas where either there are few existing instructional strategies or there are strategies that have not been tailored for particular disciplines. When this happens, and throughout an initiative, project leaders can convey to teams that they have room to *experiment*, to tinker with new strategies without the expectation of instantaneous implementation and increased student achievement. They should convey that idea testing is just that–testing new ideas to see whether they have promise for improving student literacy skills. These new strategies may or may not be immediately successful, but this is all part of the work of identifying and inventing instructional strategies that effectively serve the context, disciplinary goals, and literacy skills simultaneously.

By framing initial implementation work as a space for tinkering and finding out what works, we can ease some of the pressure associated with trying new instructional practices. Teachers in some contexts are told what and how to teach without space to exercise their expertise, and some may find it stressful to attempt practices that are sometimes unproven. In other contexts, teachers are often treated as highly autonomous, meaning they may not spend much time reflecting with others on the effectiveness of their work. In these cases, the framing of a space to tinker and try new things can be essential to helping participants attempt and then share new instructional practices.

Despite the fact that sharing new practices can be challenging, with careful planning and use of the support structures as much as possible, a team can find much work to share even if each person implements new practices at their own pace. Here is a brief overview of how each of our three core professional learning structures—PLCs, collaborative inquiry, and teacher leaders—supports the work of trying new instructional practices:

- **Teacher leaders.** Preparing teacher leaders for this varied implementation and how they might address it in their teams is important. Teacher leaders can work to normalize differences in style and implementation rate as they discuss new instructional practices. They can suggest that each teacher bring work to the group to collaboratively explore. For some teachers, this might mean bringing student work to the table following new lesson plans, but for others, getting feedback about lesson plans before implementation can be a useful way to push toward attempting new strategies. With careful management, teacher leaders can encourage implementation for participants with varied approaches to new instruction.
- **PLCs.** The PLC support structure can help provide encouragement and accountability for teachers who might otherwise be reluctant to implement new practices. By creating systems in PLCs where participants find ways to divide and conquer the workload of investigating and piloting new practices, participants can find an implementation strategy that works for them.
- **Inquiry cycles.** Because disciplinary literacy professional learning initiatives are not characterized by passing known practices to teachers, this more complex inquiry stance can actually free participants to attempt a variety of

new instructional strategies. The inquiry stance conveys a culture of experimentation and trial and error, rather than a culture of success or failure.

If a school leadership team has done the work of planning a project carefully, then these structures will help participants transition into implementation of new strategies with support. But not all inquiry cycles lead to similar types of implementation. Let's explore several common paths to implementation in the next section.

PREPARING TO IMPLEMENT NEW PRACTICES

After teachers inquire into new literacy topics and domains, they must then make the leap from learning about new ideas to trying them out in their classrooms. Too many professional learning experiences never support teachers in making this leap to testing ideas. There are a few productive pathways that teacher teams follow once they have acquired new knowledge about a topic:

- **Attempting new practices learned about through inquiry.** Sometimes teachers will inquire into a domain around which many instructional practices have been generated. Investigating topics like vocabulary tends to generate long lists of potential practices to try, and in such cases, teams must decide how they might best proceed.

  Depending on the makeup of the team and the variety of courses they teach, team members might find it best to individually identify practices to pilot in their classrooms. There might be a number of strategies being piloted simultaneously, which can lead to rich explorations of similarities and differences among various strategies and their effectiveness for students.

  Other teams might identify one or two strategies from their inquiry work to pilot. This approach focuses attention on comparing how a single strategy performs across classrooms and team members, which can be advantageous if certain practices seem especially promising to a team because of their students or their curriculum context.

- **Adapting practices for specific contexts.** Sometimes teacher teams will discover new promising practices through their inquiry work, but for a variety of reasons, they might not be able to simply insert those practices into their current classroom contexts. This sometimes happens with topics like digital literacies, wherein the structure and availability of technology in a building might shape how teachers are able to implement practices at their own sites. In other cases, a specific curriculum might necessitate tweaks to new practices in order to be fully integrated into classrooms.

In these cases, teams might decide to adapt a variety of practices, or zoom in on a limited set. Either way, team leaders and perhaps project leaders will find it important to help teachers track adaptations and effects as they attempt practices with students. Documenting successful adaptations can support later refinement and scaling of instructional strategies across content-area departments, grade levels, and schools. Consider how Jasmine Juo, from Brookline High School's Content-Area Reading Initiative, worked with her colleagues to adapt vocabulary practices for her biology classes (see the Snapshot of Practice "Adapting Practices for Biology Classes.")

SNAPSHOT OF PRACTICE
Adapting Practices for Biology Classes

During the Content-Area Reading Initiative (CRI) Summer Institute before our first year, the Brookline High School CRI Science Team decided to follow the social studies team's example and begin with a survey. We designed a six-question quiz that science students would take in class online. For biology students, we used one text from a textbook source for everyone. The result was clear and not unexpected; many students taking Biology I, a college preparatory course, had difficulty with biology vocabulary. This survey helped us to focus on vocabulary as our first inquiry cycle.

Meeting weekly with CRI science team members was critical for sharing the successes and failures of what we had experimented with in our classrooms. After reading a couple of articles about word walls, several of us tried out different methods. In my Biology I classroom, students were assigned an ecology vocabulary word to define and illustrate on blank paper. As we had more words than students, we assigned additional words to students who finished class work early. The most important work, however, occurred when students participated in small groups to organize a subset of the vocabulary words. For example, they placed words in a hierarchical order to convey meaning: population, community, ecosystem, biome, biosphere. As a whole class, we reviewed each group's work and then arranged the resulting posters on the door, keeping the word wall on display for the rest of the ecology unit.

The CRI science team decided to spend time exchanging observations with the CRI math team. I observed a math class in which the teacher had students construct a booklet that helped them define vocabulary terms and match these with examples of math problems. I quickly realized that this approach could be adapted for the upcoming cells unit for my Biology I class. Teaching cell structure and function is a challenge, as it consists of many vocabulary words that students struggle to recall, such as mitochondria and endoplasmic reticulum. I created a booklet format that organized the cell structures and had blank columns for the picture and the description. I modified an existing PowerPoint on cell organelles and printed out the slides. Students worked in assigned groups of three to five, sorting the slides into two categories, organelle pictures and descriptions, and then matching these to the correct place in the cell vocabulary booklet. Unlike when I lectured on this topic, nearly all students were engaged the majority of the time and were interacting with students in their group as well as across groups. Students prepared by reviewing the diagrams in the cell organelles textbook chapter for homework and completing a cells web quest in class. The finished product was graded and served as a study guide for the unit test. I knew that the cell vocabulary booklet was a success when a student who had performed poorly on previous unit tests, earned an A on the cell structure/function exam and cited the vocabulary booklet as helpful when studying.

~Jasmine Juo, Science Teacher,
Content-Area Reading Initiative, Brookline High School

- **Inventing practices where none are found.** Occasionally, teams will decide to inquire into a topic about which very little has been written or discovered; for example, teachers from disciplines where less has been written about literacy skills (e.g., the arts, physical education, physics, and so on). Sometimes teachers from disciplines such as math, art, or vocational fields might find far fewer suggestions for approaching literacy in their domains than teachers in fields such as English or social studies.

  Sometimes the instructional strategies they find will hint at the potential approaches they might take, but the examples given will be too far from their own subject matter and habits of mind. Instead of adopting or adapting practices, these teachers and teams need to *invent* practices themselves based on what they have learned about a domain, how it works, and how others across disciplines have approached working on those skills.

Consider the Snapshot of Practice "Piloting New Practices in Classrooms" from Marisa Olivo at the Boston Green Academy, which illustrates some of the ways in which teams pilot new ideas in their own classrooms.

SNAPSHOT OF PRACTICE
Piloting New Practices in Classrooms

In early October 2014, the urban public charter high school in which I teach, learn, and have committed years of my life to help build, learned that we were under some pressure to raise student test scores on the statewide proficiency test. Because I had been teaching tenth grade almost since the school's inception, and because I have worked to create interdisciplinary literacy projects, this hit hard. I called upon Christina Dobbs, my colleague and friend, and together we rallied for one and a half hours of team time for all tenth-grade teachers each week. We believed that working together consistently was the only way we could help our school, and our students. It turned out we were right.

Over the course of five short months of Friday afternoon meetings, our team of six tenth-grade teachers implemented solid, lasting interdisciplinary decisions about literacy, which I will briefly describe. Since this sort of professional development felt new to us, it took us a few weeks to adjust and to arrive at our first common understanding about our students and a plan to address this problem. We felt that our students often claim ownership of "already knowing" content, by stating that they "did this last year," or "we already did this math in seventh grade," or "I know how to do this."

When we pushed our students on these aspects of our individual disciplines, we felt that they actually only had a cursory understanding of the topics we were addressing. We all felt frustrated because we worked hard to plan meaningful curriculum (mostly in isolation), and some of us felt derailed by this commentary from our students. In this weekly space, we soon realized a few things: the students were doing this in all of their courses; we all felt that they didn't actually deeply understand a lot of the things they said they did; and we all weren't doing much about this because we didn't have the communal language to do so.

We also realized that addressing this problem was the first step to approaching our larger goal of improving the literacy and math skills of our students. Once we were in agreement, it wasn't long before we developed a plan. We created a heuristic as a way of communicating to our students that there is a continuum of understanding, ranging from that with which you are familiar to that which you deeply understand. We created a triangle that had the following hierarchical layers of understanding (bottom to top): I've heard of it before; I'd know it if I saw it; I can talk about it; I can explain it; and I can teach it. We decided to regularly communicate to our students across disciplines that being able to teach something to each other is the ultimate way of showing how deeply one understands a topic. The day I introduced the deep understanding pyramid to my students was the day after the last time I heard any one of them say any variation of "We already did this." This was not because I incorporated the pyramid into my classroom, but because we all incorporated it into our classrooms at the same time and with the same amount of regularity and commitment in terms of shaping lessons around this idea, using the deep understanding pyramid as a formative assessment, and making it part of lesson objectives. The pyramid wasn't just a triangle on the wall; it showed where we all placed value in learning, which is to say, we wanted more for our young people. We were no longer willing to accept cavalier claims to knowledge.

Once we saw this deeper understanding work happening, I think we started believing that we could improve students' literacy and math skills dramatically in one school year. We understood each other's stances and entry points into our collective goals, and because of that, we respected and valued each other's work more. It was easy to make and enact plans when we trusted each other's investment in the process in these meetings, in the instructional integrity of each other, in our commitment to try these practices, and in our willingness to show up each week with student work to show what we had done. In the meetings occurring after we decided upon, created, and acted out the importance of the deep understanding pyramid, we engaged in a few other key decisions: using the same mnemonic device for approaching ELA and math MCAS prompts or questions (the Massachusetts state test), agreeing to create lessons in which students used the same set of transition words from Gerald Graff and Cathy Birkenstein's 2014 book *They Say, I Say*, and a common sense of how, when, and in which capacity literacy should play a part in each core content class.

~*Marisa Olivo, Foundations of Literacy 2 Teacher,*
Tenth-Grade Improvement Project, Boston Green Academy

In each of the various paths to implementation of new practices in class-rooms (such as Marisa's "deep understanding pyramid"), teacher teams will need to rely on their previous inquiry work and their shared set of collaborative professional learning practices (e.g., structures such as discussion-based protocols) to support initial implementation. Once practices are piloted, as mentioned in chapter 8, the work is not quite finished. Teams then need to reflect on and revise those initial practices based on results of early implementation. In the next section, we discuss a variety of approaches that teams have successfully used to assess and refine new practices based on their initial work.

COLLECTING DATA TO SEE WHAT WORKS

Once teams have identified instructional practices, they need to make a plan to fulfill the next step of shared reflection and idea revision, which is the beginning of the last step in our seven-step framework. To do this, they must first assess the effectiveness of their new instruction. Teams need to determine how they will move forward to collect their own data and analyze whether new practices are affecting students. This begins what many think of as an *action research cycle*.[1] Let's review key steps in this process.

In our experience, teachers from different disciplines have been trained differently with regard to research, and they enter into *action research* with varying definitions of what constitutes evidence or data. Sometimes teachers who were trained in disciplines such as biology or chemistry have traditional definitions about experiments, and their parameters for conducting research center around features such as random assignment, features that are quite difficult for teachers to carry out in most classrooms and schools. It is important to surface these ideas early, especially when teams are interdisciplinary, and to discuss a wide variety of mechanisms that teachers can use to document the effects of new instructional practices.

The first key decision is about what types of data the team members will collect to document their new work in their classrooms. Several different types of data can be useful when reflecting, and a plan for this collection can help streamline the process. By far the most common data that teams collect are student work, samples of the tasks students complete as a result of instructional changes. But many other types of data can also be useful for assessing team work. In our work in disciplinary literacy initiatives, we have seen teams make great use of data in the form of:

- interviews and focus groups with students
- large-scale assessment data and quantitative measures
- teacher and student surveys
- video or audio footage of classrooms
- field notes, journals, or observation notes
- ancillary materials such as lesson plans or curriculum guides to study for patterns

These sorts of data can be useful, and teams should consider which will help them understand and observe student skills most closely. When teams focus on skills such as discussion, they should use a tool like video or audio footage, or detailed field notes, to document student talk as closely as possible. If they are designing a new instructional practice to help students better understand steps in a writing task, collecting student writing as well as student reflections on completing the writing tasks could be useful. Other focus domains will lend themselves to other types of data collection, and determining this in advance can help ensure that teams collect data in ways that will accurately capture changes in student learning and support team decision making regarding refinement.

In addition to determining a type of data to collect, making decisions about the logistics of how collection will occur can be helpful. For example, collecting video or audio footage can require some thought about logistics, such as a storage plan. Or collecting student work can require copying or scanning so that teachers can return original work to students in a timely fashion. If students are taking a multiple-choice assessment, then teams might consider using technology to aggregate student responses into an easily manipulatable format. Planning ahead for these logistics can help ensure that teams are well positioned to use their data, rather than having to spend too much time organizing their data for use.

ANALYZING DATA

Once data are collected, we recommend that teams adopt an inquiry stance as they begin the shared reflection process. We often use what Richard Sagor describes as the "three impact questions" as a simple tool to guide reflection.[2] The questions are:

1. What specifically did we do?
2. What improvement occurred for our students?
3. What was the relationship between our actions and changes in performance?

These three questions might seem simple, but by pushing to document broad answers to each question, teams can discern what they have learned from implementing new practices. Consider, for instance, how three teachers from Brookline High School's English inquiry team (as part of the CRI) reflected on and shared their work related to literary reading conferences (see the Snapshot of Practice "Reflecting on Reading Conference Work").

SNAPSHOT OF PRACTICE
Reflecting on Reading Conference Work

As part of an effort to explore and evaluate the different ways high school English teachers can assess what students comprehend as they read, our inquiry group looked at the reading conference model. Until we tried reading conferences, we reasoned, most of our knowledge about our students' reading comprehension came either from writing they did in response to their independent reading or from discussions of a common text with the whole class. We were looking for a way to remove writing as a variable in assessing comprehension.

For background, three of us read Patrick Allen's *Conferring: The Keystone of Reader's Workshop* and Peggy Kittle's *Book Love*. We borrowed ideas and adapted formats to use with our own students. We each conducted and recorded some sample reading conferences to share with our inquiry group. One of us recorded a student reading a passage and answering questions from a standardized test; another recorded a student reading and talking about a passage from *A Tale of Two Cities*, the current whole-class text; the third member recorded a chat with his student about a free-choice book she had been reading in class. As we listened to these recorded reading conferences together, we discussed our observations about the students' comprehension, the kinds of instruction we heard ourselves offering during the conference, and what next steps we might take with each student.

We recognized the variety of purposes that holding reading conferences could address, several going beyond just being an assessment tool. We saw how reading conferences could be diagnostic: identifying problems in accuracy, fluency, and comprehension. They could be instructional: providing opportunities to model ways for students to monitor their own reading and thinking. They could be evaluative: helping teachers determine the appropriateness of a given text for a student or class. And, beyond these purposes, reading conferences proved to be an excellent way to build relationships of trust and respect between teacher and student and build confidence in students by giving them a chance to talk about their reading with authority.

When sharing our inquiry cycle findings with our department, we offered several suggestions. To begin a reading conference, teachers might say, "Find a part that you especially loved or a part you're wondering about. Read a bit to me so that we can talk about what you're thinking." To help students monitor their own comprehension, they might say, "Tell me about some of the pictures this is passage is creating for you in your mind's eye," or "Last time we met, you mentioned you were having some trouble with some of the words or some of the language. How is that going?" or "Tell me about a time when this book has confused you and what you've done to get yourself back on track in your understanding." To use the reading conference for some instruction, the teacher might comment, "When you read that page to me, you didn't slow down at all. Remember we talked about pausing, considering, and reflecting, as we read. What would happen if you read more slowly and asked yourself some questions along the way? Or, "You seem to be having trouble reading the dialogue where two characters are talking. How about stopping periodically to make sure you know who is saying what?"

Overall, our inquiry group liked the reading conference model as an effective way to assess reading comprehension. We also recognized the challenge that holding reading conferences within class poses for teachers, including how much time can you spend with each student; what is the rest of the class doing while you are conferring; how soon can you hold a subsequent conference to address issues that surface; and how can you talk and take effective notes simultaneously during the conference? In school settings where teachers have time allotted for meeting with students outside of class, reading conferences dovetail nicely with the writing conference models that many English teachers already use extensively. Beyond their use in assessment, reading conferences can be quite valuable for providing individual reading instruction, setting reading goals, and building trust and respect between teachers and students.

~Ellen Lewis, Eric Colburn, and Julia Rocco, English Teachers,
Content-Area Reading Initiative, Brookline High School

As teachers begin the work of reflecting on their new instructional practices, we occasionally see some frustration at a lack of immediate results. For example, when teams focus on a topic such as discussion, they may feel as though students' initial discussions are not as thorough or detailed as they might like. Teams must remember that often students will need a great deal of practice with new experiences, such as discussion in the math classroom or student-led discussions in the social studies classroom, in order to become comfortable and internalize new skills.

As teams reflect on new practices, we recommend that they use a variety of discussion-based protocols to begin to make sense of what they have discovered, and to support them in making decisions about next steps. Here are a few that we have seen teams use with success, all available on the School Reform Initiative website, http://www.schoolreforminitiative.org:

- **ATLAS—Learning from Student Work.** This protocol is an excellent tool to use when initially looking at student work. The highly flexible protocol can be used in a variety of situations to look at students' work in order to understand their approaches to particular tasks, to make sense of puzzling performance, or to compare their performance across time or classrooms. It is a great tool for new teams to use to begin making sense of student work. Similarly, the Collaborative Assessment Conference can be substituted for the ATLAS, depending on the particular purposes and team needs when looking at student work.
- **The Slice.** This protocol looks at student work from several classrooms to discern patterns in teaching and learning. It requires some preparation, to sample student work from a variety of different settings, and works well when teams are all attempting to use and assess the same or similar instructional practices.

- **The Tuning Protocol.** Designed to assist teams and teachers in refining lesson and unit plans to better achieve or align with learning goals, this protocol is especially useful when teams attempt new practices that seem promising but need some fine-tuning in order to maximize effectiveness.
- **The Data Driven Dialogue or Data Mining Protocols.** These protocols are useful when teams are looking at larger data sets or even comparing sets of student achievement data. Importantly, these protocols help frame team conversations around surfacing assumptions about the data, predicting what the data might reveal, describing the data before interpreting them, asking questions about the data, noting surprises, and finally considering implications. By slowing down our natural inclination to leap from a first look at data to immediate instructional outcomes, these protocols engage teachers in a thoughtful analytic process that builds a shared understanding of how students are responding to instruction.

These protocols are a great way to begin answering the second impact question about student performance. They not only are useful for looking at student work, but can also be modified for looking at a wide range of data that a team might collect, including video footage or even student focus group data. Once some understanding of student performance has been uncovered, it is time to answer the third impact question about the relationship between what the team did and how students performed.

Sometimes teams decide to compare data collected from classrooms where new practices were and were not attempted. While this makes comparison easy, many teachers do not want to implement new strategies with only some students. In these cases, we encourage teams to consider how students seemed to struggle in prior years or units to see whether new practices are beginning to make a difference. In these cases, teams will often take the initial discussions from the protocol work they have done and consider whether they can see connections between their instructional foci and the resulting work, if they did not make explicit connections to this already. Consider how all of the elements of inquiry—designing, testing, and assessing disciplinary literacy practices—come together in the Snapshot of Practice "When Iterative Collaboration Leads to Larger Sharing" from Jenny Jacobs' work in Acton-Boxborough Public Schools in Massachusetts. Note also, how the team-level work eventually spilled over into sharing within and across schools.

SNAPSHOT OF PRACTICE
When Iterative Collaboration Leads to Larger Sharing

Going into our second year of the project, teacher teams felt a sense of urgency to see results. The reality of what deep collaborative inquiry looks like in real time began to sink in as we brought our new disciplinary literacy lens to daily practice. At times, we all felt frustrated with what seemed like the snail's pace of the work, but as the months progressed, we saw shifts in perspective take root.

One of the central topics we discussed and researched in year one was the focus on academic vocabulary. We had practiced distinguishing between discipline-specific words and general academic words ("tier three" and "tier two"). The history team, a dynamic trio of dedicated and experienced professionals, had decided to focus on this area for their inquiry work in year two. Having read about word walls in the secondary classroom, they launched into an exploration of how they might use these to support their students' learning of words from the academic word list. It wasn't long before they began to question which words were the "right" ones to focus on, and whether it made sense to have different history classes (US I, US II, World History, etc.) focus on different words. These questions led them to survey their department colleagues to get a sense of the most important general academic words for each subdiscipline. They brought their results back to the larger cohort using a consultancy protocol, after which we discussed where they might go from here. Their colleagues from the English and science teams helped them see that they had new questions about the distinction between general and discipline-specific words, which led them back to the literature and a clearer understanding of how to identify the most crucial words their students needed for success. This led them to design an informal evaluation of which words students knew from a selection of the academic word list.

This circular process of reading, working in the classroom, reflecting, and consulting with colleagues was also mirrored in our larger work, by the cohort of six disciplinary teams across middle and high school. While each team worked on the particular inquiry process we described earlier, the larger cohort also worked together to establish mechanisms for cross-disciplinary collaboration. Two examples were the schoolwide instructional fair and our own modified approach to teacher-led instructional rounds. The instructional fair, which took place during the winter of year two, was an opportunity for each team to share its disciplinary literacy work with the whole school community. Our colleagues' enthusiastic interest in the use of multiple texts, after presentations on the topic, ultimately led to a whole-school focus on using multiple texts the following fall. We also created a schedule for peer observations focused on problems of practice with a disciplinary literacy focus. Each disciplinary team defined an area of focus for its department, and we learned how to use descriptive language to observe one another and collect evidence related to the problem of practice in that department. We tried observing within high school and middle school buildings, and across buildings, and explored different approaches to debriefing these observations. What grounded this work and made it particularly helpful was the focus on the disciplinary literacy topics we had studied together. We constantly brought ourselves back to questions such as "How are tier-two and tier-three words used across history classrooms?" or "What evidence of engagement do we see when students are using multiple texts in the English classrooms?" The grounding in disciplinary literacy helped keep us focused on student learning while we added and adapted various tools to the teachers' repertoires for collaborative inquiry.

~Jenny Jacobs, EdD, Disciplinary Literacy Project Consultant, Acton-Boxborough
Disciplinary Literacy Initiative, Acton-Boxborough Public Schools

As illustrated in the Acton-Boxborough Snapshot of Practice, discussions about newly implemented disciplinary literacy practices often lead to conversations about which strategies work and for whom—with teams discovering that what works with one group or grade level does not always work the same way with another. This disparity becomes especially important as practices are shared within and across schools. Taking stock of these differences is a key component of assessing the disciplinary practices we have attempted, adapted, and invented. Now it is time to begin making decisions about what to do with what we have learned, which we discuss in the next chapter on sharing and scaling the learning from team inquiry work.

CHAPTER 10

Refining and Sharing New Disciplinary Literacy Practices

AFTER DESIGNING, implementing, assessing, and revising new instructional practices and assessments, we turn to the last piece of the sharing and evaluation phase of our seven-step framework—sharing new practices across content areas. Teams must decide how they will share their work with others. Decisions about continuing to refine practices, ending an inquiry cycle and moving on to another, and scaling practices to others outside the teams are key to ensuring that effective changes continue and spread as teams move to new focus domains. In this chapter, we explore the important decision that teams make about when and how to move from topic to topic; when and how best to share new practices developed during an inquiry cycle; and how to deepen and solidify some of the collaborative practices developed over the course of this work.

DECISIONS ABOUT MOVING FORWARD

One of the big decisions a team must make after it collaboratively pilots and refines new practices is about next steps in the team's work, and whether and how a particular inquiry cycle should end. After reflecting on the three impact questions outlined in chapter 9 and considering how new approaches played out in team members' classrooms, teams should consider next steps. Teams must decide between several different outcomes for their inquiry cycle, including:

- whether to make new instructional practices a more consistent or permanent part of the curriculum
- whether to abandon practices that did not seem to be effective or impactful
- whether to continue refining practices to better address a literacy domain
- whether to continue collecting data to better understand student performance
- whether to end an inquiry cycle to move on to another domain or inquiry topic, one of the more challenging decisions to make

In considering these outcomes, teams should remember their original purpose in selecting a topic for inquiry, which is often in response to an assessment of student needs and areas for growth.

Sometimes the initial implementation of new instructional practices yields immediate results for student learning, but when this is not the case, groups can rely on the naturally cyclical nature of inquiry and toggle back to any point in their cycle to find more ways to refine instruction or implement additional new ideas. Some groups return to reading professional texts or consulting with experts to identify additional promising practices, while others consider refining the practices they have already identified and begun to implement. Still other groups use their learning to identify a new focus domain and decide to begin a new inquiry cycle.

Any of these pathways can prove fruitful for continued work, and a few discussion-based protocol tools can support groups in making these decisions (all available on the School Reform Initiative website, http://www.school reforminitiative.org), including:

- **The Consultancy Protocol.** The Consultancy is a great tool for taking a broad look at a dilemma, such as what to do with a team's learning in the midst of an inquiry cycle. It can push groups to consider a wide array of questions and assumptions as they consider trajectories for moving forward.
- **The Charrette.** The Charrette is a powerful tool to use when teams are stuck and unsure how to move forward in their work. It identifies next steps for moving ahead with an inquiry cycle and can help groups determine a plan.

- **The Descriptive Consultancy Protocol.** This protocol is similar to the Consultancy, but it focuses more on listening and describing the current state of the dilemma. It pushes groups to fully describe what they have already done and consider that work before moving forward.
- **The Issaquah Protocol.** This protocol uses a developmental mentoring structure to shepherd a group through a description and reflection process, and then to consider new ideas for moving ahead. This generative process can lead to many concrete suggestions for moving forward.

These protocols move past the work of reflecting closely on student work and day-to-day classroom operations into the work of reflecting on bigger dilemmas and more generative ways of thinking about collaboration in the future.

The use of these tools can also help groups to identify key learnings from their inquiry cycles, effective practices that have emerged, as well as continued questions or dilemmas. An inquiry cycle is rarely finished in the sense of having all questions answered and knowing that all newly developed practices are fully effective. Yet, teams often decide (or must decide) to move on even when they leave work around a particular literacy domain unfinished, recognizing that inquiring into a new domain will likely yield insights into previous inquiries and that newly developed practices will naturally be honed and improved over time.

Teams can make decisions about the life of an inquiry cycle based on a variety of factors. These decisions are not always easy. Teams do not always find it easy to navigate whether and how to move on to new topics. Here are a few examples of considerations teams have weighed as they tried to decide when to end an inquiry cycle:

- **Seeing improvement.** Sometimes teams see improvement with their new practices and determine it is time to focus on another topic. If a team focuses on implementing a clear new instructional focus, which seems to be showing signs of success, it might then turn attention to a different area it would like to improve.
- **Finding new focus areas as a result of the current cycle.** Occasionally, a team will choose a focus domain that leads it to others. For example, a team that focused on discussion realized that students' imprecise use of vocabulary was preventing them from discussing ideas fully, so it decided to move to a cycle on vocabulary and then return to discussion.

- **Losing momentum.** Sometimes a team can do good work on a focus question or thinking in a certain domain and then lose momentum after spending awhile working on that topic. In these cases, the team might find it helpful to move on to a new topic in a new inquiry cycle in order to jump-start its thinking and renew energy. Not every cycle will lead to clear successes or to clearly apparent next steps; teams must not stall for too long in an unproductive cycle. Teams never want to lose momentum for their collaboration. Sometimes it is better to move on and then later return to a topic or inquiry cycle than to stall completely and lose interest in the larger disciplinary literacy initiative.

Teams make a variety of decisions about when to move from one cycle to another; they will do this on very different schedules. We often encourage teacher leaders to have conversations with each other to determine when to move from cycle to cycle and to help each other manage team momentum over time to keep strong collaborative improvement moving. Additionally, teacher leaders can conduct individual check-ins with team members in order to gauge their sense for when it is time to move from a particular inquiry topic. Sometimes, a team member may bring up a desire to move on that they find easier to express in one-on-one conversations than in a full team meeting.

How and when an inquiry cycle ends often signals that a team should begin thinking about whether and when to share the results of its inquiry with the broader departmental or school community. At this juncture, most teams begin discussing with whom and via which mechanisms they might engage a larger audience (e.g., grade level, department, school) in the processes and results of the inquiry cycle learning. We turn next to the issue of how and when to share newly developed ideas and practices related to disciplinary literacy.

SPILLOVER EFFECTS AND DECIDING WHAT AND HOW TO SHARE

Making determinations about work within the team and how to manage the group's timeline is only one aspect of what to consider as teams collaborate. Other important considerations are how, when, and what newly piloted instructional practices to share with colleagues outside teams, within and outside of disciplines.

As we discussed in chapter 2, professional development models often rely on spillover effects, with those engaged in professional learning efforts sharing their learning with colleagues who have not yet participated. But this sharing of new learning is difficult in schools where collaboration is inconsistent or where teachers outside the initiative are isolated. In our experience, teams need encouragement and support from their leaders as they share their work with others. In many cases, this type of sharing begins to reshape the culture of particular schools or departments, so it takes planning, care, and patience.

The first step in sharing the practices that result from an inquiry cycle is considering what to share and what to continue refining or to abandon. Here are a few questions that teams might consider as they discuss what is worth scaling to colleagues:

- Can we easily describe the new practices we have developed?
- Have we seen these new practices begin to make a difference in student skills?
- Do we think a broader community focus on these skills is worthwhile?
- Will sharing these practices start a bigger conversation about this topic across the grade level, department, or school?
- Do we think these new practices will be especially beneficial for a particular group of students?
- Could these practices support groups of students who might be struggling in doing their disciplinary work?
- Do we feel confident in our recommendation to scale a particular practice?
- Do we think a bigger discussion about this practice with colleagues might help us continue to refine it?
- Could we better support students by working on these skills using these new practices across the grades in an increasingly complex way?

Answering these questions will help teams to determine what new ideas from their inquiry cycles they are most ready to share and which are likely to have the most impact on colleagues within and across disciplines in the school. Though these questions might seem straightforward, it is important to attend to them carefully. In some instances, a team member might have tried out a newly developed idea and experienced great success with it, but this success might have occurred during only a single class session. Teams should only share new ideas and practices that are solid and well developed, or present ideas as works in progress. Teachers across the school need to build trust in the ideas emerging from a disciplinary literacy professional learning initiative. Once teams determine new practices they would like to share, then they must prepare to do so by finding an approach. Consider the quick Snapshot of Practice "Sharing the Work Beyond the Inquiry Team" from Kate Leslie, the social studies team leader for Brookline High School's Content-Area Reading Initiative (CRI) project, in which she describes a bit of the team's work creating and refining a feasible assessment and then sharing the disciplinary literacy diagnostic assessment with the larger department and school.

SNAPSHOT OF PRACTICE
Sharing the Work Beyond the Inquiry Team

When Brookline High School's Social Studies Literacy Team first convened, we didn't know what should be the focus of our literacy work. Some of us thought that our students' biggest struggles were with deciphering primary source texts. Others believed that helping students read and take notes from history textbooks was our greatest challenge. Still other group members were convinced that our students lacked the historical thinking skills needed to understand core texts. We quickly realized that we didn't know our students' literacy needs. Therefore, the group decided that we needed to develop a diagnostic test that could help us to determine students' strengths and weaknesses with literacy. This task was harder than we had imagined.

We took over a month to create a literacy diagnostic test that we trusted. First, we had to figure out which literacy skills we wanted to measure through the test. We decided to measure students' ability to:

- determine the main idea of a text
- understand cause and effect
- figure out the meaning of a word from context
- identify information in a text that's explicitly stated
- draw conclusions from implicit information

Once we determined which skills we needed to test, we still had to figure out how to do so. After many discussions, we decided that we would have students read both primary source texts and textbook excerpts that are commonly used for their grade and level. We wanted to see students' proficiency with both texts because we were unsure whether the results of the diagnostics would vary based on the type of text.

The final step of developing this diagnostic was to present it to our colleagues in the social studies department and encourage them to use it with their students, so that we would have data on every history student, ninth through twelfth grade. This posed a bigger challenge than we originally imagined because the test took an entire class period to administer; thus, some teachers felt that they didn't have the time. Furthermore, we were asking teachers to grade their own diagnostics, instead of offering to grade them ourselves. Luckily, we were able to convince our colleagues to administer the tests by stressing their helpfulness. We argued that the diagnostic would help teachers to identify students who might struggle in their classrooms; therefore, teachers could be more proactive in offering extra tutoring and help. We also believed that the diagnostic could help to identify students who were placed in the wrong academic level and might be more successful in a class that offered more one-on-one support. In the end, we were able to convince every single history teacher to administer the diagnostic test to students.

After using these tests for multiple years now, we have tweaked their format slightly. We have shortened the tests and eliminated the primary source text. We have also made the diagnostics electronic and multiple choice, so that teachers don't have to grade them and can more easily compile data for an entire grade or the entire school. But the usefulness of the tests has remained constant. These tests give teachers an early assessment of their students' literacy skills and therefore have enabled them to offer extra support to needy students, plan critical skill-building lessons for their entire classes, and encourage students who may struggle profoundly in a class to switch levels at the beginning of the year. These diagnostics have been a great aid to our teaching and have widened teachers' understanding of the literacy needs of students at Brookline High School.

~Kate Leslie, History teacher and Social Studies Team Leader,
Content-Area Reading Initiative, Brookline High School

Negotiating tensions

As teams begin to determine an approach to scaling and sharing their newly developed practices, we often find team members experiencing some anxiety about making their work public. Many different concerns can drive this anxiety, which we discuss briefly here. Some participants can feel as though they are not yet expert enough to share practices with others, especially if they are inquiring about a domain that feels very new. This stress about passing on practices that feel new, or which have been tried on a small scale but are untested at a larger scale, can make participants hesitant. Team members might grapple with any number of the following questions or concerns:

- Is it *too early* to share?
- Do we have any authority to share practices that are still quite new and perhaps not fully tested?
- How might our colleagues perceive us—perhaps as too authoritarian?
- If we don't share practices *now*, will our colleagues wonder what we've been up to in this professional learning project, and why we aren't sharing more new practices?

At this stage, many concerns (both real and imagined) can enter into the decision-making process. In many cases, we see teams feeling most unsure about how to include outsiders in a process that they experience as quite iterative, collaborative, and generative within the project. Within the professional learning project, participants have learned to expect and accept ambiguity, to live with the notion that not all practices and inquiry cycles will lead to clear outcomes. Because participants in the project have experienced a shift in mindset, to consider the work of their teams as more adaptive in nature (from chapter 4), team members often worry that just passing on packets of strategies to colleagues might result either in a misunderstanding of the broader rationale for those strategies or in no attempts to use the new practices. Several teams we have worked with have expressed concerns that if colleagues do not engage in the actual work of collaborative inquiry and piloting or refining strategies in their own classrooms, they might not truly change their instruction to improve disciplinary skills.

Beyond sharing the new, specific instructional practices, more generally, teachers sometimes hesitate to be positioned as experts in front of colleagues who share the same position within the school. In schools where collaboration is quite new, teachers might hesitate to try to influence colleagues for fear of how it might affect teamwork in the future. Less experienced teachers might feel out of place making recommendations to individuals who have been in the school for much longer, or team members might not want to do anything to influence the autonomy of others.

Teacher leaders can address these tensions, likely with support from school leaders and outside consultants. The hope is that they will be able to prompt and support teams in sharing their work. It can be smart to consider and address these concerns explicitly through discussions that reflect on potential anxieties and plans of action that take these genuine concerns into account. For example, if team members are concerned about blindly passing on the strategies with little explanation, teacher leaders can help them to plan and present their new practices with a clear rationale and description during sessions with colleagues designed for this purpose. If teams are worried about expertise, teacher leaders can help frame their work as practices uncovered by learners, rather than experts. But a key step here is to name and discuss these tensions in order to address them as teams plan the work of sharing. Following this effort, it is time to share the work of inquiry with others, in the same department, school, or even beyond.

Sharing new practices with others

A key decision in sharing inquiry work with others is to determine *what* to share from the inquiry cycle, as discussed earlier in this chapter. But, following that decision, teams must decide *who* they will share their inquiry findings and instructional practices with, carefully considering the needs of each audience. We have seen teams decide to share their work with a wide variety of groups:

- other teachers who teach a similar grade or level (e.g., tenth-grade team, honors level, etc.), or subject (e.g., chemistry, algebra, or US history)
- teachers across a whole school
- teachers who choose to come to a sharing session
- teachers across schools, such as all English language arts teachers across middle and high school or across schools in a district
- a broader group of teachers such as those attending a conference or workshop

We have seen teams share with each of these groups at different points in their professional learning process, and in doing so, several productive methods of sharing emerged. We outline these methods next:

- **Sharing through meetings.** A team could pass on its learning by hosting a training or meeting to share learning with others. We have seen groups use grade-level team meetings, department meetings, and professional development time to present both their learning process and resulting practices to colleagues.

- **Sharing through collaborative structures such as protocols.** Some teams use structured collaborations—often driven by protocols—to share their work with colleagues. As a result of inquiry work, one team from a science department developed a vertical skill sequence for literacy skills in science. Then it engaged colleagues in giving feedback on its work, and in doing so, it began a conversation about expectations and explicitness around literacy within the broader science department.

- **Involving the whole department in shared work.** Some teams choose tasks that can involve entire departments or other groups within a school in order to share the work of an initiative. One team of world language teachers focused on incorporating more reading into language classrooms. The teachers decided to build reading libraries at the end of their inquiry cycle. The team members enlisted the help of their department chair to buy new reading materials and included their whole department in selecting the materials for each teacher's classroom, not just teachers on the team.

- **Involving an administrator.** Some teams figure out ways to bring administrators into the practices that they've developed through their inquiries. In the previous example, a world language team explicitly included a department chair in the work of choosing and buying new reading materials. Gaining support and buy-in from someone in an administrative role was instrumental in supporting the full department of language teachers as they began to implement the language team's goal of supporting students in reading widely and independently as a part of learning a new language.

These strategies for sharing the work that emerged from disciplinary literacy inquiry work helped, in different ways, to engage larger groups of teachers in aspects of the collaborative work and began to engender larger conversations about disciplinary literacy within departments and schools. Not every group decides to share new instructional practices in the same way, but with careful planning, sharing can make a much larger impact beyond the team of participants. This type of work can help the effects of a disciplinary literacy initiative to truly spill over to the broader school community and even beyond.

DEEPENING COLLABORATIVE PRACTICES AND RETURNING TO THE PLANNING PHASE

As teams participating in disciplinary literacy initiatives share their work, there can sometimes be increased demand to include additional people in collaborations or to continue the conversations generated by initial participants in the initiative. In spite of what is often a desire to leap toward expanding the circle of participants when the excitement is there, in these cases, we recommend that the initial project planning team return to the planning phase of the work in order to consider building a new, expanded action space for a broader initiative. This is a natural point at which the leadership planning team can see the needs within teams and the school after having engaged in the work of disciplinary literacy professional learning for a while, as these needs have inevitably evolved over time. The leadership team can then plan how it might revise an initiative in order to meet those growing and changing needs. In particular, the sharing of practices across a school often ignites great excitement, which signals that the time is ideal to begin another phase of the initiative, inviting new teams of participants into the project in a formalized manner. Finally, the collaborative work that teams undertake often signals, across the school, the benefits of collaboration, which can push schools to consider how to make collaboration a regular, structural part of a school's schedule.

CHAPTER 11

Ending Well

All good things must come to an end.
—CHAUCER

THERE IS A VERY NATURAL, very human inclination toward wanting a project to end well. But, many of us try to avoid thinking or talking about endings. Others seek ever-elusive resolution or endings that are tied in neat little bows. All of these feelings are very natural and feel particularly true when applied to the inevitable ending of professional learning initiatives. While often success is equated with sustainability or longevity, and failure is equated with endings, we would like to offer a slightly different perspective here.

We believe that professional learning initiatives must end in order to make room for new learning and new areas of focus to emerge. Maintaining initiatives forever in the life of a school is simply impossible. The conclusion of a disciplinary literacy professional learning initiative need not be viewed as a failure or as the ending of all disciplinary literacy teaching and learning in the school. Instead, what remains can be quite powerful: a collective understanding of disciplinary literacy teaching and learning, improved ways of collaborating and learning together, and the knowledge that collaborative adult learning can indeed make a difference in student learning. All of these residuals support teachers, leaders, and students in embarking on the next dedicated professional learning venture. But, this framing of endings is quite countercultural. As we mentioned before, most people view endings negatively. Only with collective effort on the part of school leaders, teachers, and community members can a particular ending be viewed as natural, inevitable, and even celebrated.

Therefore, we end this book with a final offering, a brief chapter designed to help school leaders and teachers frame their own initiative endings, for themselves and for their communities. We offer this chapter in the hopes that your project, within your own school, may end well.

THE CHALLENGES WE FACE AND THE POWER OF ACTION SPACES

We all expect teachers in today's schools to effectively work with rapidly changing standards and increasingly diverse student populations with an enormous array of needs and interests. Teachers are expected to deliver effective instruction that suits these needs, interests, and changing standards, and to consistently incorporate new practices into their instruction. Notably, they are expected to do all of this in a world in which literacy demands are dramatically shifting. Students are expected to learn more now than ever, across a wide variety of disciplines and mediums. This challenging task requires more substantial professional learning than ever, professional learning that supports teachers in making continuous changes to instruction and assessment. No longer is teaching the same on the first day of one's career as it is on the last. If we view the task of teaching as one of continuously learning to respond to such shifts, then we must shape professional learning accordingly. All of this can overwhelm today's educators. The knowledge that today's professional learning focus may be swept aside by tomorrow's new standards or different students can leave teachers and leaders feeling less than enthusiastic about embarking on or sustaining a professional learning initiative. This is when we find it helpful to return to the notion of action spaces.

Early in this book, we discussed the idea of action spaces in education, spaces that require support and resources in order to flourish, and spaces that ultimately come to a close. In a world of continuous professional learning, with change as the only constant, the action space theory gives us a frame to focus our attention on key needs and to switch attention to other needs across time. So, when a challenge such as the increasing need for disciplinary literacy instruction arises, we can then focus on the necessary action spaces required to improve instruction to support these skills; we can intentionally assemble supports to create the conditions necessary for improvement, knowing that we will not likely need to maintain those same conditions endlessly.

Moreover, the framing of the work can include the clarity and focus that the initiative will provide. Seeking out and making the most of disciplinary literacy action spaces gives us a way to avoid dividing our attention among too many initiatives at once (one of the more common complaints of teachers and leaders in schools these days). A well-resourced action space, and one that teachers have time and energy to attend to, can produce meaningful changes in practice. This stands in opposition to what most teachers face—a litany of initiatives that pull at their time and energy, causing confusion and feelings of inadequacy. Instead, we argue that savvy leaders and teachers should frame their professional learning work in terms of action spaces, which inspire teachers to engage in deep, ongoing growth. Literacy skills are keys to success for students in and beyond secondary school, regardless of which disciplinary communities they ultimately choose to affiliate with. Therefore, we argue throughout this book that disciplinary literacy merits this sort of intense focus as a priority, within a dedicated action space.

FRAMING THE END FROM THE VERY BEGINNING

Part of ending well, with regard to disciplinary literacy professional learning initiatives, means framing the end from the very beginning. Savvy teachers and leaders will understand and talk with their community about the entire arc, or lifespan, of the initiative from the outset. Ending well means talking about the ending up front and not promising eternity through subtle omission.

Throughout this book, we have presented many stories from disciplinary literacy professional learning initiatives. In each of these cases, we saw successes both in improving literacy instruction and in teacher collaboration. Each of these schools and districts helped students to more fully access the habits of mind and ways of working for particular disciplines. These stories certainly need to be shared when designing and beginning a new disciplinary literacy professional learning initiative. But also, in truth, the action spaces that teams created for each of these projects either closed or will close at some point. We knew this as we planned and participated in the projects, and this awareness of the end allowed us to consider how schools might sustain the learning from each initiative, even as particular structures (such as weekly meetings or teacher leaders) dissolved. We urge you to share this information with your own schools and communities, too, setting the stage for ending well from the very outset.

Specific professional learning projects do end, as new action spaces open and attention turns necessarily to other areas of high need or focus. While teams may mourn the loss of a particular project, we have come to understand that new territories can be better explored because of the previous professional learning teams, collaboration, and inquiry skills teachers have acquired. We also know that resources can inevitably become scarce or dedicated to other things. We expect that this will happen in the life of any school or district as it continually works toward improvement in a variety of areas. Despite the fact that disciplinary literacy professional learning initiatives do not last forever, we count them as successes, because improved and refined literacy instructional practices and collaborative capacity are both lasting effects beyond a particular set of meetings or structures.

FINAL THOUGHTS AND WORDS OF ADVICE

What we have presented in this book is a multistep framework that we have developed over time, as schools have asked us repeatedly to help them improve literacy outcomes for their students. They often ask us to help raise literacy outcomes in secondary schools, and we have on many occasions found ourselves in conversations with school and district leaders who want to use professional learning to improve student learning as quickly as possible. We deeply identify with this sense of urgency and desire to improve outcomes for students in schools quickly. But, we have also learned that there are no silver bullets for improving student literacy. There is only the focused and thoughtful work of considering particular disciplines and particular students and fine-tuning instruction to best address this complex equation.

We sometimes feel challenged to present our framework for disciplinary literacy professional learning because, though we believe in it deeply, often our audience does not want to hear about the basis of our framework—that they should slow down and proceed carefully through the design process in order to most effectively begin the work of instructional improvement. We sometimes feel as if we are saying, "This work will be hard, will take a long time, and may involve a deep change in your school culture." Most school leaders and teachers are not eager to hear this. However, in order to see real shifts in teaching and learning, this work involves a deep investment of time and resources.

We continue to advocate for our framework because we know that isolated professional learning does not produce quick, improved outcomes. We also know that pushing against this isolated professional learning model is a leap of faith for teachers and schools that take on the complex process of improving literacy instruction. Our model is not a quick fix, but if engaged in fully and collaboratively, it will result in meaningful change that engages teachers and students in reading, writing, communicating, and thinking more deeply. Therefore, we like to think our framework is driven by urgency for deep and lasting change in literacy outcomes for students (as opposed to being driven simply by urgency for immediate change, which rarely produces the intended results).

We hope that this book has provided you with both the tools and inspiration for doing this work in your own context. We end here with a final list of important lessons learned from doing this work over the years with various schools and districts:

- **Focusing on literacy, and disciplinary literacy in particular, has great power for students as they find and pursue their own goals.** We know that many skill sets and issues are important. We have chosen literacy as our focus because we believe in its utility and power for students in school and later in life. Literacy is the toolbox for communicating in any discipline; when students have access to the language and habits of the disciplines, they can choose their own pathways as they become mathematicians or novelists or any of the variety of disciplinary careers we truly want to ensure for them.
- **Literacy is a complex and varied instructional challenge at the secondary level, and teachers will generate many of the instructional practices needed to address it effectively.** We did not begin the work of literacy improvement with schools knowing exactly what teachers from widely varied content areas would need. We have learned to look to teachers as true partners in the work of improvement, as they generate creative and thoughtful ideas for improvement that we could never have come to on our own. Their expertise is a necessary component of improvement around literacy.
- **Situating expertise across groups invests participants in the work of improvement.** Often, as we discuss projects like these with school leaders,

they ask about teachers who resist. But by carefully assembling teams and then relying on them as active participants, we find that teachers do not resist change in the ways that often accompany talk of professional learning. Instead, we see teachers finding innovative ways to make changes that fit their own classrooms and then making those changes. We also observe them developing new understandings of their own strengths and the strengths of their colleagues and taking ownership of literacy work.

- **There is never enough time.** No matter how much time we plan into disciplinary literacy initiatives, teams of teachers report that they do not have enough time to accomplish everything they would like in the given time frame. But we have learned over time to take this as a sign of investment and an opportunity to talk about priorities for instructional improvement. The goal is to make the most impactful or meaningful changes that teams can achieve in the available time, and save other changes for other times. We often remind team members that they are learning skills to come together and solve any problem or face any challenge, even once initiatives end.

- **When initiatives end, collaborative capacity skills survive.** Because we believe in action spaces, we know that the tools teachers gain for working on disciplinary literacy—collaborative conversation structures, collective problem-solving structures, team-building skills—continue to be used in the service of other improvement initiatives or in further literacy work. In this way, it is okay if a particular action space closes, as participants are better prepared for addressing and creating future action spaces. We believe in professional learning that leaves teachers better able to make improvements together as a result of their work.

- **We usually wind up somewhere somewhat different than where we thought we might.** When we partner with teams of teachers to pursue their students' most important literacy needs, we often do not foresee where we might focus our time and energy. But by setting the stage with important literacy levers for improvement and supporting team collaborations, we always find ourselves exploring rich and fertile ground with teams, even if that ground is unexpected. And in this way, teams come to serve their own needs in ways they understand deeply.

In the end, we hope this book's framework provides a useful way of considering improving literacy in secondary schools. We believe in the power of teachers to use the knowledge that they generated about literacy through research to use, adapt, and invent instructional practices that will apprentice students into their varied disciplinary communities. We hope you will take the ideas in this book and use what you can to make a disciplinary literacy initiative work in your own particular context, with all of its complexities. The journey can be long and winding. But the results—both in teacher and student learning—are well worth the trip.

NOTES

Introduction

1. We have chosen to use the pronouns they, them, theirs throughout the text in order to be gender inclusive.

Chapter 1

1. Vicki A. Jacobs, "Adolescent Literacy: Putting the Crisis in Context," *Harvard Educational Review* 78 (2008): 7.
2. Carnegie Council on Advancing Adolescent Literacy, *Time to Act: An Agenda for Advancing Adolescent Literacy for College and Career Success* (New York: Carnegie Corporation of New York, 2010).
3. Carnegie Council, *Time to Act.*
4. Christina L. Dobbs, Jacy Ippolito, and Megin Charner-Laird, "Layering Intermediate and Disciplinary Literacy Work: Lessons Learned from a Secondary Social Studies team," *Journal of Adolescent & Adult Literacy* 60 (2016): 131; Jacy Ippolito, Christina L. Dobbs, Megin Charner-Laird, and Joshua F. Lawrence, "Delicate Layers of Learning: Achieving Disciplinary Literacy Requires Continuous Collaborative Adjustment," *JSD: Learning Forward* 37 (2016): 34.
5. Timothy Shanahan and Cynthia Shanahan, "Teaching Disciplinary Literacy to Adolescents: Rethinking Content-Area Literacy," *Harvard Educational Review* 78 (2008): 40.
6. National Governors Association Center for Best Practices and Council of Chief State School Officers, *Common Core State Standards for English Language Arts and Literacy in History/Social Studies, Science, and Technical Subjects* (Washington, DC: Authors, 2010), 35.
7. Ann Marie Hillman, "A Literature Review on Disciplinary Literacy," *Journal of Adolescent and Adult Literacy* 57 (2014): 397.
8. Thomas W. Bean and John E. Readence, "Content Reading: Current State of the Art," in *Content Area Reading and Learning*, ed. Diane Lapp, James Flood, and Nancy Farnan, (Englewood Cliffs, NJ: Prentice Hall, 1989), 14; David W. Moore, John E. Readence, and Robert J. Rickelman, "An Historical Exploration of Content Area Reading Instruction," *Reading Research Quarterly* 18 (1983): 419.
9. Jacobs, "Adolescent Literacy," 19.

10. Adapted from Doug Buehl, *Developing Readers in the Academic Disciplines* (Newark, DE: International Reading Association, 2011).

11. Richard D. Vacca and Jo Anne L. Vacca, *Content Area Reading*, 7th ed. (Boston: Allyn & Bacon, 2002).

12. Candace S. Bos, Patricia L. Anders, Dorothy Filip, and Lynne E. Jaffe, "The Effects of an Interactive Instructional Strategy for Enhancing Reading Comprehension and Content Area Learning for Students with Learning Disabilities," *Journal of Learning Disabilities* 22 (1989): 384; Steven V. Horton, Randall A. Boone, and Thomas C. Lovitt, "Teaching Social Studies to Learning Disabled High School Students: Effects of a Hypertext Study Guide," *British Journal of Educational Technology* 21 (1990): 118; Jeffrey M. Lederer, "Reciprocal Teaching of Social Studies in Inclusive Elementary Classrooms," *Journal of Learning Disabilities* 33 (2000): 91.

13. Gina Biancarosa and Catherine E. Snow, *Reading Next—A Vision for Action and Research in Middle and High School Literacy: A Report to Carnegie Corporation of New York* (Washington, DC: Alliance for Excellent Education, 2004); Carnegie Council, *Time to Act*; Mark Conley, "Cognitive Strategy Instruction for Adolescents: What We Know About the Promise, What We Don't Know About the Potential," *Harvard Educational Review* 78 (2008): 84.

14. Leigh A. Hall, "Teachers and Content Area Reading: Attitudes, Beliefs and Change," *Teaching and Teacher Education* 21 (2005): 403; David G. O'Brien and Roger A. Stewart, "Preservice Teachers' Perspectives on Why Every Teacher Is Not a Teacher of Reading: A Qualitative Analysis," *Journal of Reading Behavior* 22 (1990): 101; David G. O'Brien, Roger A. Stewart, and Elizabeth B. Moje, "Why Content Literacy Is Difficult to Infuse into the Secondary School: Complexities of Curriculum, Pedagogy, and School Culture," *Reading Research Quarterly* 30 (1995): 442; Ned Ratekin, Michele L. Simpson, Donna E. Alvermann, and Ernest K. Dishner, "Why Teachers Resist Content Reading Instruction," *Journal of Reading* 28 (1985): 432.

15. Larry D. Yore, "Secondary Science Teachers' Attitudes Toward and Beliefs About Science Reading and Science Textbooks," *Journal of Research in Science Teaching* 28 (1991): 55.

16. K. Denise Muth, "Reading in Mathematics: Middle School Mathematics Teachers' Beliefs and Practices," *Reading Research and Instruction* 32 (1993): 76; Roger A. Stewart, "Factors Influencing Preservice Teachers' Resistance to Content Area Reading Instruction," *Reading Research Quarterly* 28 (1990): 55; Sam Wineburg, *Historical Thinking and Other Unnatural Acts* (Philadelphia: Temple University Press, 2001).

17. Elizabeth B. Moje, "Foregrounding the Disciplines in Secondary Literacy Teaching and Learning: A Call for Change," *Journal of Adolescent & Adult Literacy* 52 (2008): 96.

18. Jeffery D. Nokes, *Building Students' Historical Literacies: Learning to Read and Reason with Historical Texts and Evidence* (New York: Routledge, 2013); Cynthia Shanahan, "How Disciplinary Experts Read," in *Adolescent Literacy in the Academic Disciplines: General Principles and Practical Strategies*, ed. Tamara Jetton and Cynthia Shanahan (New York: Guilford, 2012), 69.

19. Elizabeth B. Moje, "Developing Socially Just Subject-Matter Instruction: A Review of the Literature on Disciplinary Teaching," *Review of Research in Education* 31 (2007): 1; Elizabeth B. Moje, "Doing and Teaching Disciplinary Literacy with Adolescent Learners: A Social and Cultural Enterprise," *Harvard Educational Review* 85 (2015): 254.

20. Cynthia Shanahan and Timothy Shanahan, "The Implications of Disciplinary Literacy," *Journal of Adolescent and Adult Literacy* 57 (2014): 629.

21. Bill and Melinda Gates Foundation, *Teachers Know Best: Teachers' Views on Professional Development* (Seattle: Bill and Melinda Gates Foundation, 2014); Hilda Borko, "Professional Development and Teacher Learning: Mapping the Terrain," *Educational Researcher* 33 (2014): 3.

22. Zhihui Fang and Suzanne Coatoam, "Disciplinary Literacy: What You Want To Know About It," *Journal of Adolescent & Adult Literacy* 56 (2013): 627.

Chapter 2

1. Hilda Borko, "Professional Development and Teacher Learning: Mapping the Terrain," *Educational Researcher* 33 (2014): 3; Linda Darling-Hammond, Ruth Chung Wei, Alethea Andree, Nikole Richardson, and Stelios Orphanos, *Professional Learning in the Learning Profession: A Status Report on Teacher Learning in the United States and Abroad* (Stanford, CA: National Staff Development Council, 2009).

2. Sharon Feiman-Nemser, "From Preparation to Practice: Designing a Continuum to Strengthen and Sustain Teaching," *Teachers College Record* 103 (2001): 1013.

3. Bill and Melinda Gates Foundation, *Teachers Know Best: Teachers' Views on Professional Development* (Seattle: Bill and Melinda Gates Foundation, 2014).

4. Borko, "Professional Development and Teacher Learning," 3; Richard F. Elmore, *School Reform from the Inside Out: Policy, Practice, and Performance* (Cambridge, MA: Harvard Education Press, 2004).

5. Thomas R. Guskey and Kwang Suk Yoon, "What Works in Professional Development," *Phi Delta Kappan* 90 (2009): 495.

6. Gates Foundation, *Teachers Know Best.*

7. Megin Charner-Laird, Monica Ng, Susan Moore Johnson, Matthew A. Kraft, John P. Papay, and Stefanie K. Reinhorn, *Gauging Goodness of Fit: Teachers' Assessments of Their Instructional Teams in High-Poverty Schools* (working paper, Harvard Graduate School of Education Project on the Next Generation of Teachers, Cambridge, MA, 2016); Joan E. Talbert, "Professional Learning Communities at the Crossroads: How Systems Hinder or Engender Change," *The Second International Handbook of Educational Change*, ed. Andy Hargreaves, Ann Lieberman, Michael Fullan, and David Hopkins (New York: Springer, 2010), 555.

8. Feiman-Nemser, "From Preparation to Practice," 1013.

9. Michael S. Garet, Andrew C. Porter, Laura Desimone, Beatrice F. Birman, and Kwang Suk Yoon, "What Makes Professional Development Effective? Results from

a National Sample of Teachers," *American Educational Research Journal* 38 (2001): 915; Ben Jensen, Julie Sonnemann, Katie Roberts-Hull, and Amélie Hunter, *Beyond PD: Teacher Professional Learning in High-Performing Systems* (Washington, DC: National Center on Education and the Economy, 2016).

10. Richard DuFour, Rebecca DuFour, Robert Eaker, and Thomas Many, *Learning by Doing: A Handbook for Professional Learning Communities at Work* (Bloomington, IN: Solution Tree, 2006); Kevin Fahey and Jacy Ippolito, "Variations on a Theme: As Needs Change, New Models of Critical Friends Groups Emerge," *JSD* 36 (2015): 48; Karen Seashore Louis, Sharon D. Kruse, and Anthony S. Bryk, "Professionalism and Community: What Is It and Why Is It Important in Urban Schools?," in *Professionalism and Community: Perspectives on Reforming Urban Schools*, ed. Karen Seashore Louis, Sharon D. Kruse, and associates (Long Oaks, CA: Corwin, 1995), 1; Louise Stoll, Ray Bolam, Agnes McMahon, Mike Wallace, and Sally Thomas, "Professional Learning Communities: A Review of the Literature," *Journal of Educational Change* 7 (2006): 221.

11. Talbert, "Professional Learning Communities," 555.

12. Gates Foundation, *Teachers Know Best.*

13. Talbert, "Professional Learning Communities," 555.

14. Dufour et al., *Learning by Doing*; Matthew Ronfeldt, Susanna Owens Farmer, Kiel McQueen, and Jason A. Grissom, "Teacher Collaboration in Instructional Teams and Student Achievement," *American Educational Research Journal* 52 (2015): 475; Talbert, "Professional Learning Communities," 555.

15. Vivian Troen and Katherine C. Boles, *The Power of Teacher Teams: With Cases, Analyses, and Strategies for Success* (Thousand Oaks, CA: Corwin, 2012).

16. Stoll et al., "Professional Learning Communities," 221; Nancy Fichtman Dana and Diane Yendol-Hoppey, *The Reflective Educator's Guide to Professional Development: Coaching Inquiry-Oriented Learning Communities* (New York: Corwin Press, 2008).

17. Dana and Yendol-Hoppey, *Reflective Educator's Guide,* 50.

18. Dana and Yendol-Hoppey, *Reflective Educator's Guide.*

19. Marilyn Cochran-Smith and Susan L. Lytle, *Inquiry As Stance: Practitioner Research for the Next Generation,* (New York: Teachers College Press, 2009).

20. Cochran-Smith and Lytle, *Inquiry As Stance*; Michele D. Crockett, "Inquiry As Professional Development: Creating Dilemmas Through Teachers' Work," *Teaching and Teacher Education* 18 (2004): 609; Ronald Gallimore, Bradley A. Ermeling, William M. Saunders, and Claude Goldenberg, "Moving the Learning of Teaching Closer to Practice: Teacher Education Implications of School-Based Inquiry Teams," *Elementary School Journal* 109 (2009): 537; Garet et al., "What Makes Professional Development Effective?"

21. Dan Clement Lortie, *Schoolteacher: A Sociological Study* (Chicago: University of Chicago Press, 1975).

22. Tamara Holmlund Nelson, Angie Deuel, David Slavit, and Anne Kennedy, "Leading Deep Conversations in Collaborative Inquiry Groups," *The Clearing House* 83 (2010), 176.

23. Alma Harris, "Teacher Leadership: More Than Just a Feel-Good Factor?," *Leadership and Policy in Schools* 4 (2005): 201; Alma Harris and Daniel Muijs, *Improving Schools through Teacher Leadership* (London: Oxford University Press, 2004); Institute for Educational Leadership, *Teacher Leadership in High Schools: How Principals Encourage It, How Teachers Practice It* (Washington, DC: Institute for Educational Leadership, 2008); Jennifer York-Barr and Karen Duke, "What Do We Know About Teacher Leadership? Findings from Two Decades of Scholarship," *Review of Educational Research* 74 (2004): 255.

24. Janet C. Fairman and Sarah V. Mackenzie, "Spheres of Teacher Leadership Action for Learning," *Professional Development in Education* 38 (2012): 229.

25. Gates Foundation, *Teachers Know Best*; Jensen et al., *Beyond PD*.

26. Diane Yendol Silva, Belinda Gimbert, and James Nolan, "Sliding the Doors: Locking and Unlocking Possibilities for Teacher Leadership," *Teachers College Record* 102 (2000): 779; York-Barr and Duke, "What Do We Know?"

27. Fairman and Mackenzie, "Spheres of Teacher Leadership"; Harris and Muijs, *Improving Schools*; Jason Margolis, "Hybrid Teacher Leaders and the New Professional Development Ecology," *Professional Development in Education* 38 (2012): 291.

Chapter 3

1. Charles M. Payne, *So Much Reform, So Little Change: The Persistence of Failure in Urban Schools* (Cambridge, MA: Harvard Education Press, 2008).

2. Joseph P. McDonald and the Cities and Schools Research Group, *American School Reform: What Works, What Fails, and Why* (Chicago: University of Chicago Press, 2014).

3. McDonald, *American School Reform*, 22–23.

4. McDonald, *American School Reform*, 23.

5. McDonald, *American School Reform*, 23.

6. Dan C. Lortie, *Schoolteacher: A Sociological Study* (Chicago: University of Chicago Press, 1975).

7. Timothy Shanahan and Cynthia Shanahan, "Teaching Disciplinary Literacy to Adolescents: Rethinking Content-Area Literacy," *Harvard Educational Review* 78 (2008): 40.

8. Christina L. Dobbs, Jacy Ippolito, and Megin Charner-Laird, "Layering Intermediate and Disciplinary Literacy Work: Lessons Learned from a Secondary Social Studies Team," *Journal of Adolescent & Adult Literacy* 60, no. 2 (2016): 131–139.

Chapter 4

1. J. Ippolito, A. Breidenstein, F. Hensley, and K. Fahey, "An 'Uncommon' Theory of Educational Leadership: Preparing Leaders Who Can Facilitate Transformational Change in Schools" (paper presented at the annual meeting of the American Educational Research Association, San Antonio, Texas, April 2017).

2. Ron Heifetz, Alexander Grashow, and Marty Linsky, *The Practice of Adaptive Leadership: Tools and Tactics for Changing Your Organization and the World* (Cambridge, MA: Harvard Business Press, 2009).

3. Heifetz et al., *Practice of Adaptive Leadership*.

4. Victoria Gillis, "Disciplinary Literacy: Adapt Not Adopt," *Journal of Adolescent & Adult Literacy* 57 (2014): 614.

5. Heifetz et al., *Practice of Adaptive Leadership*.

6. Joseph P. McDonald and the Cities and Schools Research Group, *American School Reform: What Works, What Fails, and Why* (Chicago: University of Chicago Press, 2014).

Chapter 5

1. Rita M. Bean and Jacy Ippolito, *Cultivating Coaching Mindsets: An Action Guide for Literacy Leaders* (West Palm Beach, FL: Learning Sciences International, 2016), 218–200.

2. Bean and Ippolito, *Cultivating Coaching Mindsets*, 159–162.

3. Bean and Ippolito, *Cultivating Coaching Mindsets*, 159–162.

4. Kathy P. Boudett and Elizabeth A. City, *Meeting Wise: Making the Most of Collaborative Time for Educators* (Cambridge, MA: Harvard Education Press, 2014); Joseph P. McDonald, Nancy Mohr, Alan Dichter, and Elizabeth C. McDonald, *The Power of Protocols: An Educator's Guide to Better Practice*, 3rd ed. (New York: Teachers College Press, 2013).

5. Megin Charner-Laird, Jacy Ippolito, and Christina L. Dobbs, "The Roles of Teacher Leaders in Guiding PLCs Focused on Disciplinary Literacy," *Journal of School Leadership* 26, no. 6 (2016); Christina L. Dobbs, Jacy Ippolito, and Megin Charner-Laird, "Layering Intermediate and Disciplinary Literacy Work: Lessons Learned from a Secondary Social Studies Team," *Journal of Adolescent and Adult Literacy* 60, no. 2 (2016): 131; Jacy Ippolito, Christina L. Dobbs, and Megin Charner-Laird, "Bridge Builders: Teacher Leaders Forge Connections and Bring Coherence to Literacy Initiatives," *JSD: Learning Forward* 35 (2014): 22; Jacy Ippolito, Christina L. Dobbs, Megin Charner-Laird, and Joshua F. Lawrence, "Delicate Layers of Learning: Achieving Disciplinary Literacy Requires Continuous, Collaborative Adjustment," *JSD: Learning Forward* 37 (2016): 34.

6. Charner-Laird, Ippolito, and Dobbs, "Roles of Teacher Leaders."

Chapter 6

1. Megin Charner-Laird, Jacy Ippolito, and Christina L. Dobbs, "Teacher-led Professional Learning," *Harvard Education Letter* 30 (2014): 8; Jacy Ippolito, Christina L. Dobbs, and Megin Charner-Laird, "Bridge Builders: Teacher Leaders Forge Connections and Bring Coherence to Literacy Initiative," *JSD: Learning Forward* 35 (2014): 22.

Chapter 7

1. Timothy Shanahan and Cynthia Shanahan, "Teaching Disciplinary Literacy to Adolescents: Rethinking Content-Area Literacy," *Harvard Educational Review* 78, no. 1 (2008): 40.
2. Shanahan and Shanahan, "Teaching Disciplinary Literacy."
3. Dan Clement Lortie and Dan Clement, *Schoolteacher: A Sociological Study* (Chicago: University of Chicago Press, 1975).

Chapter 8

1. Marilyn Cochran-Smith and Susan L. Lytle, *Inquiry as Stance: Practitioner Research for the Next Generation* (New York: Teachers College Press, 2009).

Chapter 9

1. Nancy Fichtman Dana, *Digging Deeper into Action Research: A Teacher Inquirer's Field Guide* (Thousand Oaks, CA: Corwin Press 2013).
2. Richard Sagor, *Collaborative Action Research for Professional Learning Communities* (Bloomington, IN: Solution Tree, 2010).

ACKNOWLEDGMENTS

THERE ARE MANY PEOPLE who made contributions to this book, and to our professional lives, that we would like to thank here.

First, we must thank all of the teachers, students, and school leaders who we have worked with in disciplinary literacy professional learning initiatives. They have taught us so much about how to collaborate in powerful ways. Witnessing their amazing dedication to supporting students reminds us of what is possible with great enthusiasm and innovation.

We would particularly like to thank those who contributed their experiences to this volume: Mary Angione, Eric Colburn, Ann Collins, Brooke Feldman, Jenny Jacobs, Jasmine Juo, Ellen Lewis, Kate Leslie, Joanna Lieberman, Brenna Mahoney, Shelley Mains, Marisa Olivo, Julie Padgett, Philip Pietrangelo, Jenee Ramos, Julia Rocco, and Gary Shiffman. Your stories are the heart of this book.

Additionally, many people have mentored us and shaped our thinking about this work over the years.

Christina would like to thank Catherine Snow, Paola Uccelli, Nonie Lesaux, Pamela Mason, Scott Seider, and all her colleagues at BU who have encouraged this work. She is especially grateful to her community on the BU SED Equity, Diversity, and Inclusion Committee for their work toward justice.

Jacy would like to thank Catherine Snow, Nonie Lesaux, Richard Elmore, Joshua Lawrence, Vicki Jacobs, Pamela Mason, Kevin Fahey, Frances Hensley, Angela Breidenstein, Gene Thompson-Grove, and Cami Condie and his many colleagues at Salem State University and the School Reform Initiative who continue to shape his thinking and work.

Megin would like to thank Susan Moore Johnson, Kay Merseth, John Diamond, and her many inspiring colleagues from the Project on the Next Generation of Teachers who helped to shape her as a researcher. Additionally, thanks to her colleagues at Salem State and beyond for their partnership and for continuing to support and influence her work.

We thank the editors and staff at Harvard Education Press for their support and guidance throughout this process.

We are thankful to have found each other as colleagues, coauthors, and friends supporting one another along our journeys through academia.

We thank our families and friends for supporting us always.

And finally, we are grateful to all of our current and former students, who renew our energy and sustain our desire to support teachers in making powerful change in schools.

ABOUT THE AUTHORS

CHRISTINA L. DOBBS is an assistant professor in the English Education program at the Boston University School of Education in Boston, Massachusetts. Christina's research focuses on disciplinary literacy and academic language, the development of adolescent writing skills, and the professional learning that supports teachers in these areas. Christina is particularly interested in effective disciplinary instruction for students who are diverse along a variety of dimensions and the potential of teachers to enact effective instruction for all students. Her work has been published in journals including *Reading Research Quarterly*, *Written Communication*, the *Journal of Adolescent & Adult Literacy*, and *Applied Psycholinguistics*. Christina was an editor of the volume *Humanizing Education: Critical Alternatives to Reform*. She earned her master's and doctorate degrees at the Harvard Graduate School of Education, is a literacy coach and reading specialist, and began her teaching career as a high school English teacher in Houston, Texas.

JACY IPPOLITO is an associate professor and department chair in the School of Education at Salem State University, Salem, Massachusetts. Jacy's research, teaching, and consulting focus on the intersection of adolescent and disciplinary literacy, literacy coaching, teacher leadership, and school reform. Jacy is especially interested in the roles that teacher leaders, literacy coaches, and principals play in helping institute and maintain instructional change at middle and high school levels. The results of Jacy's research and consulting work can be found in a number of journals and books, including the *Journal of Adolescent & Adult Literacy*, *Professional Development in Education*, the *Journal of School Leadership*, the *Journal of Staff Development*, and *The Elementary School Journal*. His recent books include *Cultivating Coaching Mindsets* (2016), *Adolescent Literacy in the Era of the Common Core* (2013), and *Adolescent Literacy* (2012). Jacy completed his master's degree and doctorate in language and literacy at the Harvard Graduate

School of Education. Prior to his work in higher education, Jacy worked as a middle school reading specialist, literacy coach, and drama teacher in Cambridge, Massachusetts.

MEGIN CHARNER-LAIRD is an assistant professor in the School of Education at Salem State University, Salem, Massachusetts, where she also serves as the Lead Faculty for Assessment. Megin's research and teaching focus on the ways that teachers learn and grow as professionals, how they respond to policy enactment, and how teacher leadership can serve as a lever for improvement in classrooms and schools. Megin's work puts teachers at the center and is premised on the belief that teachers have the capacity to develop and enact the changes necessary to improve teaching and learning for all students. Megin's research and writing have been published in a number of journals, including *Teachers College Record*, the *Journal of School Leadership*, *Educational Administration Quarterly*, the *Journal of Adolescent & Adult Literacy*, *Professional Development in Education*, and the *Journal of Staff Development*. She served as an editor of *Education Past and Present: Reflections on Research, Policy, and Practice*, a volume celebrating the seventy-fifth anniversary of the *Harvard Educational Review*. Megin completed her master's degree and doctorate at the Harvard Graduate School of Education. Prior to her studies there, she taught elementary school in California's Bay Area.

ABOUT THE CONTRIBUTORS

Mary Angione was the science team leader in the CRI project at Brookline High School. She is currently a chemistry teacher at BHS.

Eric Colburn was a member of the English team in the CRI project at Brookline High School. He is currently an English teacher at BHS.

Ann Collins was a member of the social studies team in the CRI project at Brookline High School. She is currently a librarian at BHS.

Brooke Feldman was a team leader and participant in the One Dorchester Project when she was a teacher at Boston Collegiate Charter School. She is currently a social studies curriculum coordinator (grades 6–8) in the Needham Public Schools in Needham, Massachusetts.

Jenny Jacobs, EdD, was an expert consultant on the Acton-Boxborough DL Project. She is currently an assistant professor at Wheelock College in Boston.

Jasmine Juo was a member of the science team in the CRI project at Brookline High School. She is currently a biology teacher at BHS.

Ellen Lewis was a member of the English team in the CRI project at Brookline High School. She is currently retired from BHS.

Kate Leslie was the social studies team leader in the CRI project at Brookline High School. She is currently a history teacher at BHS.

Joanna Lieberman was on the planning and design team and is an administrative support team member for the middle school disciplinary literacy project in the Brookline middle schools. She is currently the English/Language Arts K–8 Curriculum Coordinator for the Brookline Public Schools.

Brenna Mahoney was a member of the hybrid team focused on multitiered student support services in the CRI project at Brookline High School. She is currently a special educator at BHS.

Shelley Mains was a member of the world languages team in the CRI project at Brookline High School. She is currently a librarian at BHS.

Marisa Olivo was a member of the tenth-grade improvement project team at Boston Green Academy. She is currently a foundations of literacy teacher at BGA and a doctoral student at the Lynch School of Education at Boston College.

Julie Padgett was the math team leader in the CRI project at Brookline High School. She is currently a math teacher at BHS.

Philip Pietrangelo was an environmental science teacher and a member of the tenth-grade improvement project team at Boston Green Academy. He is currently a science teacher at Boston Latin School.

Jenee Ramos was the English team leader and project manager of the CRI project at Brookline High School. She is currently an English teacher and Dean of Faculty at BHS.

Julia Rocco was a member of the English team in the CRI project at Brookline High School. She is currently an English teacher at BHS.

Gary Shiffman was on the planning and design team for the CRI project at Brookline High School. He is the Social Studies Curriculum Coordinator at BHS.

INDEX